Surviving Loss and Finding Magic in the Missing

KELSEY CHITTICK

ISBN: 978-1-951407-49-0 paperback

ISBN: 978-1-951407-43-8 ebook

DISCLAIMER

This work is non-fiction and, as such, reflects the author's memory of the experiences. Many of the names and identifying characteristics of the individuals featured in this book have been changed to protect their privacy, and certain individuals are composites. Dialogue and events have been recreated; in some cases, conversations were edited to convey their substance rather than written exactly as they occurred.

To Jack and Addison. May you always remember that you were born from a beautiful love story. Your dad accomplished a lot in 42 years, but nothing was as important or meant more to him than being your father. You're the reason I will always live in gratitude and joy.

CONTENTS

Introduction ix

PART I
The Beginning 1

1. The Story of Us 3
2. Football & Friends 23
3. Fly Me to the Moon 35
4. Truth & Vasectomies 50
5. Saying Goodbye 60
6. Angels & Airports 71
7. Morgues & Miracles 78
8. Memories & Memorials 91
9. Coroners & Coffee 104
10. Helmets & Heartaches 110

PART II
The Healing 119

11. Dark Nights 121
12. The Therapy 127
13. Present Moments 138
14. Reframe or Go Insane 146
15. Talk to Me 153
16. I'm Enough 160
17. The Journey 165
18. Concussions & Crying 185
19. Gratitude & Joy 197
20. Fly Free 205
21. Moving Forward with Hope 209

Epilogue 215

Notes 221
Acknowledgments 223
About the Author 229

INTRODUCTION

"There are only two ways to live your life: as though nothing is a miracle, or as though everything is a miracle."

– Albert Einstein

I had 12 grief books on my nightstand, seven lasagnas in my refrigerator, two sobbing kids and one dead husband.

It was a cold, dark afternoon in November. I was in bed wearing mismatched Target pajamas and staring at my ceiling fan. As the fan went around and around, I tried to keep my eye on *one* paddle as some sort of weird mental game, but I kept getting distracted by all the dust on each blade. "Someone should clean that," I thought. But I couldn't move. I had no energy and no hope. The only thing I could do was lay there, staring at the fan and thinking to myself, "Holy shit, we are so screwed."

A few days before, on November 11, 2017, my amazing husband—a seemingly healthy and strong retired NFL player and Super Bowl champion—had died of a massive heart attack at the age of 42 in front of my kids.

Suddenly, my whole world felt surreal. In one moment, my kids lost their dad, and I lost the man I had loved for 21 years. I was 40 years old, and now I was a widow with two kids. My life was unrecognizable. We went from a life we loved to a new life that was unwanted, unimaginable and more painful than we thought we could handle.

This story is about traveling from that journey into a new reality. It's about holding on, letting go and ultimately enjoying the ride. This is the story of endings and beginnings and how change can be both heartbreaking and healing at the same time. A lot of it is painful, and some of it is funny, but most of it is simply magical.

This journey felt the way I imagine surviving a natural disaster would feel. One minute, life is calm and familiar; the next, everything looks and feels totally different. I lost all sense of comfort and security. In the time it takes for one heart to stop beating, I was thrown into the unknown, where pain and joy, sorrow and gratitude, mix together. And in that moment, I was forced to face myself and who I wanted to be in this new life. I had to decide if I was ready to do the hard and beautiful work each of us is eventually called to do.

I dove into books, articles and podcasts about death because I was desperate to connect with other people who had lost someone they loved. I needed to know that this was something people could survive. I journaled about what I learned and clung to the words and stories people shared. Their insights and experiences became the guides I followed along the way.

I also sobbed uncontrollably, rubbed my legs until they bled, took Xanax and lay for hours on my bathroom floor. I was looking for relief in every area of my life. Each night, I lay in bed and watched my thoughts loop over and over in a continual cycle of "How could this happen?" and "Why did he die?" and "How will we go on?" I struggled to understand how he was no longer living in my home or alive in this world.

For a while it felt like nothing was helping.

But after about three months, once the gut-wrenching holidays were behind us, I felt something start to change. I was in the kitchen crying, as usual, when my daughter Addison walked in. It was a few days before her 10th birthday.

"Mom, are you okay?" she asked.

I looked down at myself and realized the answer was "No." I looked like someone with a meth habit: dirty robe, hair in a greasy bun, swollen eyes.

Addison asked again, "Mom, are you okay? Have you been crying again?"

I nodded, and she grabbed my hand. "Mom, please," she begged. "I don't want you to be sad anymore. I just don't want everything to be so sad anymore."

At that moment I realized that our house used to be the most joyful place. Before Nate died, there were parties and dancing. Our home had been filled with laughter and friends for 15 years, and now it seemed painfully quiet.

We were all desperate to have happiness back in our lives, but I didn't know how to do that *and* feel all the pain. How can I be joyful *and* broken at the same time? I decided I would have to fake it a little and see if that could move us in a different direction.

"Alexa, play 'Three Little Birds' by Bob Marley," I commanded our favorite Amazon assistant.

My daughter looked stunned. It had been a while since we had listened to music.

"Alexa, volume eight!" I yelled.

As the music began to fill our kitchen, a small smile came over Addison's face. We looked at each other, laughed, and began to dance around the kitchen island, just like the old days.

Don't worry about a thing

'Cause every little thing gonna be alright

Singing' don't worry about a thing

'Cause every little thing gonna be alright

My son Jack walked in, sleepily rubbing his eyes. When he saw us twirling around the kitchen, he looked shocked—like he couldn't understand what was happening. But then his face relaxed, and he smiled.

"You know you two are crazy, right?" he said, then turned to go back to his room. When I think back to what I saw on his face that day, it was relief.

For the first time in months, I had some space from the pain. And most importantly, I had laughed with my kids. In the beginning, grief is all-encompassing and, most of the time, completely out of your control. But there are always small breaks in the pain, little slivers of hope that show up each day. From that point on, we started to recognize those moments, and instead of ignoring them, we began to walk towards them.

After that day, I started wearing the robe less often, even though many days it still hung on me like an old friend. Every week I tried to wash and dry my hair at least once. On some days, that simple task felt like an Olympic event. Even though I only took Ambien once a week, I knew it was time to stop. There were times that I missed the blackout sleep, but once I was off of Ambien, I started to dream more. And some of those dreams began to blissfully include Nate.

I worked hard not to feel sorry for myself. I would say into the mirror, "Okay, I give up. I'm here and ready to experience this whole thing and see where it takes me. I won't decide if it is good or bad—I'll just accept it and ride the waves of emotion as they come."

I didn't do this because I was brave or special; it was because I was desperate. I knew the only other option was to give up, fall apart and decide that the whole thing wasn't worth the pain. So almost three months after Nate's death and a few days before my daughter's 10th birthday, I made a conscious choice about how I would experience, share and live through my loss. I did it for my kids and for me and because I wanted to make Nate proud.

If you knew Nate, you would understand that his dramatic exit was exactly how he would have wanted to die: jumping and laughing with his two kids, the people he loved the most in the world—until suddenly, just like that, he was gone. I'm sure no one was more surprised than Nate. I can imagine him suddenly floating out of his body toward the light, saying, "Wait, what—Now? Oh, wow. Okay—Hold on." I imagine he was torn between staying here and transitioning to the Divine. I will never know what he felt in those last moments, but I trust that at some point, he was overcome with a feeling of peace and a great sense of amazement. I want to believe that he whispered, "Oh, God, this is beautiful. I'm going home." And just like that, he was off into another realm.

Nate embodied the saying, "Go big or go home!" He simply *loved* everything about life. Each meal was his favorite, every conversation was important and his gratitude was contagious. He was huge, both physically and in the way he lived. So, in his honor, I went big on experiencing his death. I was determined to make sure that although they had lost their dad, my kids wouldn't lose me. I began to train my heart, my mind and my soul to view our experience in a totally different light. And that made all the difference.

Because of the way I shifted my mindset, this is not a book about grief and loss; this is a story about life and living fearlessly. It's a story about choosing joy, not only when times are good, but (especially) when times are gut-wrenchingly hard. It's about connection and community and how, when you share the pain, the load gets lighter. It's about finding humor and joy in between the darkest moments. It's about leaning into the pain and then letting it all go. It's about looking at death in a totally different way and ultimately realizing that you never lost anything—it just got transformed.

Losing Nate has been the hardest and most painful experience of my life. Yet at the same time, this has been the most beautiful and magical time of my life. I would do anything to have him back for one more day or even one more minute, but I know that isn't how this story is supposed to go. I wouldn't wish my experience on anyone—and I wouldn't trade it for anything.

PART ONE
THE BEGINNING

ONE
THE STORY OF US

"My mission in life is not merely to survive but to thrive; and to do so with some passion, some compassion, some humor, and some style."
– Maya Angelou

Nate and I had a great marriage. We laughed, we fought, and we hugged all the time. We both truly enjoyed each other's company, and we also both loved being apart. We loved getting in bed together at night, and we treasured sleeping in separate beds when we were on vacation. Overall, we were very happy.

But of course, like every marriage, there was room for improvement. There were many days when I would text my best friend and say, "I swear I'm going to kill that man!" or "You will never believe what he did!" But like all of us who love someone, I didn't want him to die. I just wanted him to take out the trash, remember to get milk and drink five fewer beers on a Sunday.

When I was overcome with love for him, or in moments when I felt overwhelmed or scared, I would say to him, "Please don't forget that you're my best friend. You are my favorite person, and I can't do this without you." He would look me in the eyes and promise that he never would leave.

When I get to Heaven and find him (most likely in a sports bar watching the Yankees, surrounded by women of all races and nations), I will have words for him.

One of the hardest parts about losing Nate was that nobody knew me the way he did. He knew my hands were rough and that I had a hidden bald spot on my head. He knew my heels didn't touch the ground when I peed ("Hey, why are you on your tippy toes? Put your feet down, weirdo!" he would joke when he walked in unannounced). We grew up together. We had exceptional kids together. He thought I was funny and annoying, bossy and beautiful. We argued often, laughed every day and loved each other with great passion. At the end of our arguments, he would give me a hug and say, "There is no one else I would want to hate."

And we weren't just soulmates; we also had a mind-blowing sex life. Okay, that was a lie, but he would have loved for me to write that—I can feel him high-fiving me from Heaven as I type. Truth is, we were married. And our sex was—very married. Meaning we did it in the same position for about 10 minutes, give or take. But we did it a few times a month, so I consider ours to be a great love story.

IT WAS the spring of 1997. I was sitting at a bar in Chapel Hill, North Carolina, called Four Corners. It was a popular sports bar at the far end of Franklin Street where a lot of the athletes hung out. During my senior year in high school, I had been recruited by several colleges for swimming. Chapel Hill had been my first choice, and I felt lucky to be a part of the University of North Carolina women's swim team. My teammates and I decided to head over to our favorite bar with the hopes of meeting some hot lacrosse or soccer players.

But on this particular night, we had just heard that most of the lacrosse team was going to some house party. We kept looking around to see if any cute guys were going to show up or if we needed to change locations. My girlfriends and I were sitting shoulder to shoulder at the bar trying to figure out if ordering another round of Long Island Ice Teas would make us "too drunk" or "just drunk enough." Around 9 p.m., the door opened, and in walked a group of UNC football players. These guys were so enormous that it took my breath away. I leaned over to one of my friends and asked, "Can you imagine dating these guys?! Way too big!"

As the large men filed in, some of them began to walk

toward our group. There was clearly no room for them at the bar, but they didn't seem concerned. It seemed as if they were used to getting their way; some of them just leaned over us to order their drinks. I recognized a few of the guys because one of our teammates, Tracey, was dating a guy named Ryan on the offensive line.

Suddenly an enormous blond man slid in behind me and politely yelled to the bartender in a Philly accent, "Yo, good friend! Could I get a beer? I'm dying of thirst over here."

I had to scoot close to my friend because this guy took up a lot of space and seemed unaware of his physical size. He grabbed his beer, put a $20 bill on the bar and took a huge sip. Then he turned to us.

"Well, hello ladies. Don't you all look stunning tonight?"

We all laughed.

"And what are the names of these beautiful women?" he continued.

We introduced ourselves, and then one of my friends asked, "And you are....?

He responded, "Nate Hobgood-Chittick."

I laughed out loud. By the way he said it, I couldn't tell it was hyphenated. "Hobgoodchittick" all ran together like a nonsense word. I thought he was joking. That name didn't match this big, husky blond Scandinavian man in any way.

"Are you for real?" I asked him. "Please tell me how someone that looks like you has a name like that."

He took another sip of his drink and scooted in a little closer. "Well, it's a long story, but you can basically blame it on my mom. She's smart, but she's also very intense *and* a huge feminist."

I liked the sound of her.

"So, what does that have to do with such a long last name?" I asked. He explained that she wanted him to have both her last name and his father's last name, but she'd waited to ask Nate if that was okay with him.

I was confused. "Wait, you chose this name?" I asked. "You like it?"

"No, I hate it!" he confessed. "It's ridiculous. Barely fits on my jersey. But yes, I agreed to it. Probably because she asked me when I was seven!"

I laughed and thought, "What an interesting guy. But what a rough last name."

Nate went back to his friends while my group closed out our tab. As I stood up from my barstool, Nate walked over and slid a napkin in front of me. He gestured for me to open it, and I saw that he had written a note. It said, "*If you want the best, say goodbye to the rest. Go home with me, and I'll make you happy.*"

I thought it was a joke and turned around to say something funny, but he was already walking away.

"Nate Hobgood-Chittick!" I called out. He slowly turned around. I held up the napkin and shook my head laughing. With a sweet smile on his face, he winked at me and walked away.

Even though it would be months before I would see

him again, I never forgot that first meeting. Something about him stayed with me, in my soul; I knew it wasn't the last time our paths would cross.

THAT SUMMER I spent breaking up and getting back together with Derek, my boyfriend of two years. I had met him at the beginning of my freshman year. He was on the men's swim team at UNC and struggled with a weed and drinking problem. I knew he wasn't right for me for numerous reasons. Not only was he emotionally unavailable, but there were a number of other red flags as well. For example, he crashed his parked motorcycle into his neighbor's car while drunk. And his whole apartment had wicker furniture. Anyone who thinks it's comfortable to watch TV on a wicker couch is not right in the head.

One Sunday, right before the start of my junior year, he called and said, "We need to talk."

From the minute he walked in, I could smell the aftermath of 18 holes of golf and a boozy brunch.

Even though he was far from perfect, he had helped me through some rough times during my freshman year. I knew we weren't meant for each other, but I still cared for him.

"I'm sorry Kelsey, but I met someone else," he said. "We fit better; she's more fun and laid back than you."

I thought, "Well, pretty much everyone I've ever met

is more laid back and fun than me, so that's not surprising."

Still, I wanted a few more details. "Where did you meet her?" I asked.

He told me that she was a hostess at the Chili's in Durham, where he would always get breakfast after playing golf.

After he left, I slunk to the floor of my bedroom and ticked off the events of the last two years. My parents were getting divorced, and my brother was going through some challenging times. My performance in the pool was declining, and my scholarship was on the line. I was racing terribly—my times were getting slower due to low effort in practice—and I had gained 15 pounds as a result of my newfound love of croissants with cream cheese. Once Derek cheated on me with the "fun" hostess at the Durham Chili's, I knew something needed to change.

"Sweet baby Jesus, Lord have mercy," I said out loud to myself. "This is a low point in my life."

I knew that this was the wake-up call I needed. I was tired of feeling overwhelmed and sad. All these events combined showed me that I was making bad choices and not doing well when it came to dealing with hard times. I needed to get my life back on track. So I grabbed my journal from under my bed and started to write down exactly what I wanted out of my life. I was 20 years old, and I wanted to get clear on who I was and where I wanted to be. But I needed some help.

Hey God—so, I need a little help. Been doing life my

way for a while, and it isn't going very well. Time to put you back in charge. Good news is I know who I want to be and what I want out of life, but I have no clue how to get there. I'm trusting you have a plan. My best thinking got me to this point, so I am going to let you take it from here. I'm done trying to figure it out.

Sorry it took me so long to reach out. Thank you. Love you God.

After that, I visualized everything I wanted in life: joy, laughter, success, passion, great friendships and an enlightened man that was confident, kind and spiritual. Someone who wanted to live an exceptional life and would encourage me to do the same.

Looking back, I don't remember asking for a huge defensive lineman from Allentown, Pennsylvania, with a chewing tobacco problem and premature balding, but that was exactly who showed up—again.

IT WAS the fall of 1997, and football was in the air. The swimming and football seasons were in full swing, and both teams were having exceptional years. One of my roommates, Liz, was dating Chris Keldorf, a talented and attractive quarterback from Carolina who was leading the Tar Heels to a record-setting year. One Sunday night, Liz suggested that Chris bring some of his friends over to our house, Old Pit, where we lived with three other girls from the swim team.

Their recent success made them seem like celebrities, and we were excited they were coming to party with us. We dressed in our best Abercrombie outfits and waited.

When the doorbell rang, tall, skinny Chris walked in first; behind him came the rest of the offensive line, large beefy men who took up most of our entryway. Then, trailing behind everyone else, there was a guy I recognized from a bar I had been in months ago, wearing jeans and a FUBU sweatshirt.

I thought to myself, "Whoa, it's Huge-Blond-Dude-With-The-Weird-Last-Name."

As Nate sauntered in, he looked around with a serious face, politely introducing himself to everyone. He then headed to the kitchen and immediately began to make himself at home. He opened doors, cabinets and the refrigerators. He didn't stop in the kitchen, either, but slowly walked around the entire house, peering into every room. It was as if the house was telling him something.

As the night went on, the party got into full swing. Everyone was laughing, watching *The X-Files* and enjoying a plethora of drinks. At some point, I went to my room to get something, and Nate walked in behind me.

I looked up. "Hello? Are you looking for the bathroom?" I asked.

He shook his head and answered, "Nope, just checking the place out."

Normally it would have been weird or even alarming to have a large man I didn't know in my bedroom, but for some reason it wasn't. I could tell he was a good guy, overly curious and a bit socially awkward, but harmless. He looked around and stopped when his eyes landed on the Serenity Prayer that was hanging on my wall.

He read it quietly to himself: "God grant me the serenity to accept the things I cannot change, the courage to change the things I can and the wisdom to know the difference." When he was done, he looked at me with the sweetest face and said, "I live my life by that shit."

I was blown away. Not because of what he had said, but because in some deep way, I knew that this was the man I had been waiting for my whole life.

That first Sunday night, after *The X-Files* ended, we cranked up the countertop CD player and blasted Michael Jackson. Everyone was on their way to a big night and an even bigger hangover. At some point, Nate, who was dripping with sweat, picked up an empty Coors Light box and put it on his head. He had been solely responsible for finishing the beer and spent the rest of the evening using the box as a hat.

Around 11:30 p.m., a guy I had been dating from the Naval Academy called our home phone. As I talked to him, Nate looked over at me from the middle of the kitchen, where he was perfecting his signature hip thrusts. He calmly walked over, asked who it was and then took the phone from my hand. He politely said to the guy, "Hey, buddy. No need to call anymore—she's with me now." And then he flexed his bicep, winked at me and headed back to dance.

I turned to my roommate and exclaimed, "What a weirdo! Who does this guy think he is?!"

But there was a twinkle in his eye that made me trust him—despite his size, his house roaming and even his overly confident and forward courting habits. When I checked in with myself, I knew I would see him again.

Nate called me every day after that, leaving long slow messages on our shared home answering machine. One day, after the sixth message was left, my roommates had heard enough. They encouraged and then begged me to call him back; they were tired of listening to his messages. That night when I called him, we ended up talking for hours. I was surprised by how natural our conversation felt. And I now truly understood his "never quit" attitude.

Eventually, I agreed to go out with him but not before I grilled him about his courting tactics. "You do know you have really bad manners and come on super aggressive?" I asked him over the phone. "You realize that you can't just walk into my room without permission, right? And the way you talked to my boyfriend, even if he is a loser, was very rude."

He listened quietly and then replied, "My apologies, I can see how that was all a bit much and over the top. I'll work on doing better. I'm so sorry. Now, do you want to go out with me on Friday?"

I can't remember if I said yes that night or a few weeks later, but eventually we went out during the day. He asked me to join him for lunch after class at Subway.

After we ordered our six-inch sandwiches, we slid our way down to the register. Nate insisted that he pay, but when the man ran his card, it was declined.

"That's impossible!" Nate asserted.

The clerk ran it again, but it still didn't work. I quickly handed over my card, paid the $11 bill and walked outside to meet Nate, who by then was pacing and screaming up at the sky. "Why me? Why are they doing this to me again!?"

I had no idea what he was talking about or who "they" were, but I knew he was terribly embarrassed. He calmed down as we started to walk back to campus.

"Kels, I have *no* idea why there wasn't any money left on that card!" he said. "It's crazy!"

I asked him if maybe he just made a big purchase or needed to increase his limit. He responded that he hadn't bought anything recently, and his limit was $2,500.

I was shocked—that seemed so high for a college kid. At the time, my limit was $500, and I had never felt so rich.

"Nate, what the hell have you bought that maxed out the $2,500?" I asked.

"It's probably maxed out because of these goddamn parking tickets," he said. "They keep towing me *for no reason*!"

I was confused. How many tickets could a college kid get before changing his behavior?

"Why don't you put more money in the meter or set your watch for the days there's street sweeping?" I asked.

"That's not the issue," he said. "No matter what happens, if I park in this one spot, they tow me."

"What spot?" I continued to probe.

"Well, it's the Chancellor's spot," he replied. "But I only park there when it's empty and he's not using it! I don't see what the big deal is."

I knew then that this man was special in both good and bad ways.

On our first official evening date, we got fancy. He picked me up in his seafoam green Taurus, which I could tell he had cleaned that day. He opened the door for me, and when I sat down in the car, I saw what looked like a bullet hole in the windshield.

"What caused that?" I asked, pointing to the spot.

He barely glanced at it and replied, "Not sure. But don't worry, it's all good."

I so badly wanted it to be a rock. The thought of dating someone who had been shot at—or even worse, had been shot at and didn't remember—made me feel uneasy. But I put it out of my mind and focused on the piña colada scented air freshener that was hanging on his rearview mirror. That smell, combined with the extremely generous amount of Drakkar Noir cologne he was wearing, was making me feel lightheaded.

His outfit that night could best be described as "comfortable": XXL sweatpants and a fitted blue T-shirt from Old Navy. It was tight in a way that made his arms look strong and his belly look—big. This would essentially be his uniform for the rest of his life.

He and I were a lot of things, but "best dressed" was never an award that would be bestowed upon us. For this evening, I had carefully chosen baggy Ann Taylor shorts and Birkenstocks. We probably both thought we looked fantastic. The scary part was that those outfits were the best either of us had to offer.

We drove up to Franklin Street, the main spot in Chapel Hill, and walked up the stairs to Top of the Hill—one of the best restaurants around campus, mostly because it has gorgeous views of the entire college. Nate found us a high-top outside, away from everyone, and we sat and talked for hours. I noticed that his intensity was high, his pauses were long and his desire to find the meaning of life was deep. I had never experienced someone listening to me so intently in my life.

Towards the end of the evening, he said, "We should dance." It was an odd request because there wasn't a dance floor, and I could barely hear the music. I thought, "Is this guy for real? Why does he want to dance?"

It felt strange, yet something in my gut said, "Just go with the flow." I wasn't a "go with the flow" type of girl so that thought took me by surprise. Normally I would have pushed back with a bunch of questions and judgments and recommendations, but for some reason, I was intrigued. And what I learned that night was that Nate truly didn't care what anyone thought. He did what he felt and, on this night, he wanted to dance. It seemed to be a refreshing way to walk through life—and one I had never experienced before.

We sauntered out onto the invisible dance floor, and although I could barely reach his neck with my arms, we stood out there all alone and swayed around. After a few songs, he excused himself and went to the bathroom.

While he was gone, some fraternity guys I knew walked over and asked me if we were dating.

I answered yes, and they laughed.

"Wow, you two look like Beauty and the Beast," one of them said.

When the guys walked away, I wondered if I should tell Nate what they had said, but I didn't know how he would react. In the end, I told him anyway.

After I shared what they had said, he glanced over to the guys at the bar. Then he gave me a big hug and whispered into my ear, "Don't you ever let anyone call you 'beast' again."

I fell in love with him that night. Maybe it was his sweet face, his 291-pound body or the fact that he had a voice that reminded me of a porn star. Whatever it was, I was in for the long haul.

For the next few weeks, we spent as much time together as we could between school and our respective football and swim practices. Once I felt we were committed, I decided to tell some of the girls on the team as we sat around in the locker room after practice. One of the seniors overheard the conversation and said, "Wait, did you say Nate Hobgood-Chittick?"

I nodded.

"*That* guy has been with everyone!" she exclaimed.

Typically, that would have bothered me, but because Nate and I had already deeply explored these topics, it didn't upset me at all.

When I'd asked him at dinner one night how many people he'd slept with, he was very upfront, and I think simultaneously proud and slightly embarrassed by the high number. We were opposites in that category, but his honesty and the way he explained it, along with his insistence that I was the woman he had been waiting for, made me feel safe.

After that conversation, I never felt jealous or insecure. Not in college, not when he played in the NFL, not at any time in our life together. It felt like once we found each other, he changed, and his only focus was on me. (If after this book comes out, I find out he has an illegitimate child, just forget about this part of the story.)

Once we started dating, everything in my life got better. I swam faster, and my grades improved. It felt like his love made me believe in myself. He said, "You can do anything if you work hard!" And so I did. He told me I could earn a full scholarship if I put my mind to it. And I did that too. He was my biggest fan, always reminding me I was capable of great things.

During my junior year, our team was traveling to the conference championship at the University of Virginia. It was the culmination of the season and determined how we ranked in our conference and which individual swimmers and relays would go on to the national NCAA meet in March. My teammates and I loaded our bags under the bus and were getting situated for the long drive when I looked outside and saw Nate pulling into the parking lot. There were no other boyfriends around, and all the girls started messing with me.

"Hey girl! Ohh, loooooook who came to see you!"

Nate walked onto the bus, said hello to all the ladies as if he owned the place and walked up to my seat. He leaned over and gave me a kiss before handing me two things: a cassette tape and a tiny spark plug that he brought from the gas station he worked at during the summer.

But the spark plug wasn't the normal metal color; instead, he had hand-painted it baby blue and white, the colors of the University of North Carolina.

I was confused. "A spark plug?" I asked. "A cassette tape? Thank you?"

He leaned against the seat with all the confidence and swagger in the world and said slowly, "You are my spark plug; it'll remind you how fast you are. The music is for the ride; it has all my favorite songs on it." I felt very loved.

As the bus pulled away, he stood in the parking lot and waved goodbye. I blew him a kiss and put the tape into my Walkman. Putting my headphones on, I closed my eyes and started to listen to the first song. He had recorded himself saying, "This is my favorite song, and it makes me think about you." The song was "I'll Be Missing You" by Puff Daddy and Faith Evans. It wasn't until 21 years later that I truly understood why it was meant for me.

With Nate's encouragement, I had the best swim meet of my career. As I stretched on the pool deck before the finals of the 200-yard backstroke, I knew I had a chance to do well. My body and mind were calm as the referee said, "Take your mark," and the start gun went off.

Every moment of that race felt good. At the 100-yard mark, I could see I was still racing with the leaders and knew that it would come down to the final 50 yards. My legs were on fire, and my heart felt like it might explode, but I also felt stronger than ever. As I hit the final turn, I knew it was time to go. I pushed off the wall and kicked harder than ever before. I swam that last lap with everything I had, and when I hit that wall, I knew I had given it my best. I looked up to the scoreboard, and a huge smile spread over my face. I looked over at my coach and my teammates and pumped my fist in the air.

That day, I swam the fastest time of my life and got second place in the event. With that personal best time, I was now ranked top 30 in the country and qualified to compete in my first national collegiate championship meet. Making it to that meet had always been my final goal, and I knew that Nate's encouragement and confidence had made it possible.

I was still in my junior year, but Nate's collegiate career was coming to a close. He had just finished his final season and his senior year at UNC and didn't know what his future looked like. Since he had arrived at Carolina five years earlier, Nate had spent most of his time playing backup defensive tackle. Over the years, he had many opportunities to make plays during practice but very little field time during the games. That year, UNC had produced some of the best defensive linemen in the country. Although he was playing very well, many of the coaches didn't think he would ever have a chance to play football professionally. He wasn't the fastest or the most talented. But he was a hard worker and a leader among his teammates.

The year before, after his junior season, Mack Brown, the head coach of the football team, asked Nate into his office. He said, "Listen Nate, you have four All-American defensive tackles playing in front of you, and you aren't playing much. I think you should quit and get ready to go to law school."

Mack wanted to give his scholarship to someone else and knew Nate had been interested in law as a career after he was done playing football. Nate was heartbroken by the conversation, so Mack agreed to give him one more chance.

"Nate, if you have a great spring season and prove yourself again in practice, you can keep your scholarship and play your senior year."

In true Nate fashion, that spring he worked his ass off every day and fought to keep his scholarship. He often told me, "That was the worst conversation I ever had, but it motivated me to work harder." He hated that his coach didn't believe in him, but he had also been very clear. "Nothing is going to keep me from being a part of the team," he said. "I don't quit. Ever."

That year, both Nate and I had received the "Most Improved" award for our respective teams.

Something had shifted for both of us, and I knew we made each other better. Good things were starting to happen.

TWO
FOOTBALL & FRIENDS

"The difference between a successful person and others is not a lack of strength, not a lack of knowledge, but rather a lack of will."

- Vince Lombardi

The NFL Draft took place in April of 1998, right after Nate's senior season. It's the biggest day for football players who have dreams of playing in the NFL; all over the country, players and their families get together to watch the seven rounds of the draft and hope that their player would get picked up by a team.

A group of us met up at Chris Keldorf, Jeff Saturday and Nate's house to watch the event live. In the beginning, everyone was hopeful that all of them would be picked up. But as the hours went by, the phone didn't ring. As each round of the draft came to a close, the mood got more and more somber. Once it was over, everyone just looked shocked. Not one of them had been picked to try out or play for a team.

Then out of the blue, 20 minutes after the draft ended, the phone rang. Everyone suspected they were calling for Jeff Saturday or Chris Keldorf; both had exceptional careers and record-making statistics. Maybe a team wanted to pick them up as free agents and give them a chance to make their team?

Jeff answered the phone.

"Hello, can I please speak to Nate Hobgood-Chittick?" said a scout from the New York Giants.

Jeff smiled and handed Nate the phone. Even though Jeff wanted an opportunity to play in the NFL, he was also Nate's biggest fan and thrilled they had called for Nate. We watched as Nate ran up the stairs and closed his bedroom door to continue the conversation.

About 15 minutes later, he came down the stairs and said quietly, "I'm going to the New York Giants. They're giving me a shot to make the practice squad. My sign-on bonus is $5,000 and a case of beer!"

Everyone cheered and hugged Nate. Chris and Jeff put their hopes for themselves aside and were proud of Nate. He had worked so hard, and today, that work paid off.

Nate was thrilled, but he also deeply wanted his buddies to take this next step with him; all he ever wanted was for everyone to win together. I could tell he was struggling. And although he was excited, he was even more nervous about what it would take to get to the next level.

Still, he was convinced no one could stop him. "Babe, I have a chance to play football, in the NFL, in the greatest city in the world," he told me. "They'll have to drag me out of there in a body bag because I'm never going to quit."

That day changed his future trajectory, and that phone call would affect his life in both amazing and devastating ways.

Four months later, Nate went to Giants training camp. He was thrilled to have a chance to play in the NFL, but to play in New York, so close to his Allentown friends and family, was almost too good to be true.

His parents had recently relocated from Allentown to Boston as both of them began new jobs. His dad was the campus pastor at Harvard University and ran the University Lutheran Church. One of his passion projects was running the Harvard Square Homeless Shelter with his congregation and student volunteers. Nate's mother was a Religious Ethics professor in the Theology Department of Holy Cross in Worcester, Massachusetts. His brother had just graduated high school and was on his way to the University of Massachusetts, where he played on the football team for four years. Nate was back in the northeast, the part of the country he would always call home.

Training camp was hard for him that first year. He

was in constant pain, literally screaming every morning as he heaved himself out of the bed. Once he got moving or took a warm shower, he felt better, but the pain was always there—he could barely move his fingers because the joints were locked, and his arthritis had gotten worse. After a sleep test with the Giants medical team, he was diagnosed with sleep apnea and began using a CPAP machine at the age of 22; he never slept without it again. His whole body had issues, but he tried not to complain. When he would see me sitting cross-legged on the floor, he would say, "Kels, my knees would explode if I tried to sit like that!"

Even though I was still in my senior year of college and swimming for UNC, I drove up to New Jersey after practice each Saturday to help him settle into the little rental house he shared with two other guys. I felt so grown-up as we walked the aisles of Ikea and bought beds and dressers. One day we spent over $500 on particle board furniture, which, at that time, felt like a fortune.

"That was a lot of money," Nate said when we got in the car. "We need to be careful because at any point, I could be cut by a team. Most likely, I'll never make more than the league minimum, and that's only on the weeks I play."

There is a misconception about the salaries of professional athletes, especially NFL players. Of course, there is a small percentage of players who sign multi-million-dollar contracts and are, hopefully, set for life. But most players live paycheck to paycheck, trying to stay on a team and play each week so they can get paid. Football careers are also notoriously short, averaging only three years. Nate was very aware that we needed to save whatever he made because we never knew when this journey would be over.

His favorite statistic to share with people was that 70 percent of guys in the NFL end up broke or divorced (or both) once they retire. He knew of so many players who had lived beyond their means and ended up in tragic places. He was committed to that not happening to us. I had grown up in a financially comfortable but very frugal family, so this made perfect sense to me. I was grateful that, from the start, we almost always agreed on the financial side of our relationship.

Our goal was to save enough money for a down payment on a house and hopefully put some away to invest. We didn't spend much on anything, including Nate's car. When all the other guys were buying tricked-out Escalades and driving Mercedes sedans, Nate went *way* far in the other direction.

During his career, he drove a practical and very unattractive maroon conversion van. I'm not a high-maintenance person, but even for me, this was a stretch. Once, when I pulled up to the players parking lot gate in Kansas City, the guard stopped me and eyeballed the van.

"I'm sorry Miss, but this is the parking lot for players and their wives," he said. I pulled out my pass and ID, and he let me through, looking very confused.

That day, after our trip to Ikea, we got back to his

rental house with all the furniture, and I laid everything out in an organized manner. This is where I shined. There must have been 72 screws, 12 shelves, 19 washers and 98 tiny nails. Nate looked overwhelmed, and I could tell this wasn't going to be an easy project for him. We divided up the furniture this way:

Kelsey: one coffee table, two shoe racks, one dresser, one kitchen table, four dining chairs, one bed frame.

Nate: one bedside table.

I watched Nate struggle with simply opening the box and finding the instruction sheet. I was in the zone and fast at work when I heard Nate talking to himself.

"This is ridiculous! They give you directions, but there are *no words*! I have no fucking idea what these stick figures are telling me to do!"

He was sitting uncomfortably on the floor with four table legs and a tabletop, losing it.

"I'm missing so many pieces!" he yelled.

I replied back in my most encouraging voice, "Everyone feels that way when they start. Don't give up sweetie."

But it was too late; he was already tapping out. "Sorry babe, but my back and knees are on fire, I have a headache and I need a nap," he said.

As he slowly moved his leg to stand up, I saw a washer stuck to the back of his leg.

"There's your missing piece," I said and winked at him.

From that point on, he spent the day being more of a

cheerleader and less of a contributor when it came to furniture assembly.

When I finally got tired and climbed into bed for a nap, he said, "Thanks for your help. I'm so lucky to have you in my life." He kissed me on the cheek. Then he added, "After this, let's only buy furniture that comes assembled. Okay?"

Soon after, Nate survived a brutal training camp and made the Giants roster. For three weeks, he pushed his body and his soul in ways he didn't know were possible. Every night we would talk on the phone and review the day. "Kels," he would say, "I have never been in this much pain. Everything hurts; I can barely move. Sometimes I literally feel like my heart is going to explode. But if I let up, someone else will get my job."

At the end of Giants camp, after Nate had made the team, he called his younger brother Luke to share the great news. "Luke! I made the mother fucking team! But I'm going to tell you something, that shit was brutal. We had to run on the treadmill for an insane amount of time at a speed I didn't think was possible. I told myself, 'There are only two ways you are coming off—either dead or because you made the team.'"

I was worried about him because he always sounded so exhausted and in pain. But he kept saying, "Don't worry. I just try not to think about it. I want to make this team." He was convinced that if he could play for a few years and save some money, it would give us a great start in life.

Nate's career started with the Giants, but he never played in a game with them. After a few months in New York, he got cut from that team and picked up by the Indianapolis Colts. Once he got to Indianapolis, he worked hard to make the team and find his place on the field. The whole time he was practicing against his teammates on the offensive line, he kept thinking about his college roommate and best friend, Jeff Saturday. After playing against guys in the NFL, Nate knew Jeff had what it took to be a part of a team. He wanted to help him.

After practice one day, Nate decided to go talk to Colts general manager Bill Polian. Nate walked in wearing dirty sweats and said, "There's a guy selling electrical supplies in Raleigh right now who whipped all those first-round draft choices at North Carolina every day." Nate asked if Jeff could come up to Indianapolis and be given a shot to play.

Polian looked at him and said, "I love it. Let's get him in here for a workout."

The next week, Jeff moved in with Nate, and the rest is history. Jeff went on to spend 13 seasons in the NFL, win a Super Bowl with Peyton Manning and play in six Pro Bowls. His name is in the Colts Ring of Honor, and he has been nominated for the Pro Football Hall of Fame.

As Jeff has said many times, "There aren't many people in the world who would go to bat for you like that —especially in his position because he didn't have any leverage."

Soon after, Nate was released from the Colts. He wasn't sure where he would go next, but then he received a phone call from the St. Louis Rams. Their head coach, Dick Vermeil, had seen Nate's work ethic during a training camp scrimmage and thought he could be a good addition to the team. It turned out to be an exceptional year to be a part of that team. In 1999, Nate played in his first and only Super Bowl.

During that magical season with the Rams, Nate's last name became something special. During pregame warmups, the entire team chanted his name as their rallying cry—50 men of all races and backgrounds in a tight-knit circle screaming, "Hobgood-Chittick!!! HOBGOOD-Chittick!" at the top of their lungs. It was partly because they liked the way it sounded and partly because of what he meant to the team: he was a hard worker, he never gave up and he believed everyone had something to give.

After the Rams won the NFC Championship and were headed to the Super Bowl in Atlanta, Nate was excited. But not just for himself—he was thrilled to have his friends get to share this once-in-a-lifetime game with him. During the weeks before the game, he became stressed. Everyone thought it was about the game, but I knew he was most worried about making sure all the people who were coming had a great time.

"Kels, do you think they're going to be okay with the room we got?" "I'm so overwhelmed with the logistics of all the people!" "I wish I had more tickets to the after-party." "How do I handle the seats?" "Who goes where?" These questions kept him up at night because he didn't just want to win for himself; he wanted to win for all his friends and family. He was singularly focused on giving them the best experience they could have in Atlanta. He wanted everything to be perfect--which also meant he deeply wanted to win.

The 1999 Super Bowl was one of the best games ever played. The Rams played the Tennessee Titans and had a 9-0 lead in field goals at halftime. In the third quarter, they scored the game's first touchdown, making it 16-0. In response, the Titans scored 16 points to tie the game with 2:12 minutes left in regulation time—the biggest point deficit ever covered in Super Bowl history at that time. After that, the Rams completed a monster 73-yard pass to take back the lead, 23-16. In the fourth quarter, the Titans drove all the way to the 10-yard line and had six seconds left on the clock. The whole game would come down to the last play. After the snap, Titans' quarterback Steve McNair completed a pass to receiver Kevin Dyson, who then charged towards the end zone—until Mike Jones, the Rams' linebacker, wrapped him up and brought him down at the one-yard line in a moment so dramatic, it has since gone down in NFL history as simply "The Tackle." With no time left on the clock, the Rams had won their first Super Bowl since 1951.

The Rams had won, and the entire stadium went crazy.

I was both shocked and ecstatic. As I stood in the

stands, I cried for Nate and all the hard work it took him to get there. I was overjoyed for the team, which was made up of some of the most exceptional men I have ever met. The players' bodies were broken and tired; they had pushed themselves to the limit. During this season and this game, they ignored injuries and concussions while fighting mental and physical exhaustion. But on this one night, it all must have seemed worth it for them. Nate and his teammates were World Champions.

Coach Vermeil was someone Nate looked up to his entire life. Not only was he a great coach, but there was an honesty and kindness to him that Nate deeply admired. The feeling was mutual. When talking to a reporter about Nate, Coach said, "I almost immediately started developing a fondness and respect for him because he was one of those extremely high-effort guys no matter what you were doing. He had a hard time going slow on a walk-through." Nate was all-in, all the time, and on this particular night, it had paid off.

Along with an overwhelming sense of joy, I was also very relieved. Relieved that the season was over, and he didn't have to play football for a while. I felt that way after every play, every game and every season. I wanted Nate to be healthy and safe, and on a deep level, I was aware that although the sport was giving us a lot, it might be taking even more.

After the game ended, a huge celebration began on the field. We watched as Nate and his teammates ran around hugging each other and lifting each other into the air. After about 10 minutes, Nate looked up into the stands where we were all waiting. There was a huge group that included me, his dad, his brother and his best friends from college, high school and childhood. He pointed to us and pumped his fists into the air, then ran toward us. I smiled because I knew he was going to jump into the stands and run into my arms, just like in the movies.

He somehow pulled his 300-pound body up over the railing and was heading to my section. But right before he got to me, he veered left and ran into the arms of his best friends. I thought, "Wait, I'm over here! You were supposed to come hug me!"

But watching him celebrate with his friends, I remembered exactly why I loved him so much. Nate and his buddies had dreamed about winning a Super Bowl since they were kids. I, on the other hand, had never thought about it a day in my life. And in all honesty, I'd never even watched a game until I started dating Nate. What I loved about that moment is that Nate could have run to me and done what I thought he *should* do, but instead, he followed his heart. Those friends were the ones who had been with him from the beginning, and he needed them to know how much he valued and loved them. That day, he ran to the right people. The mental picture of all of them celebrating together in the stands is still one of my favorite memories from that game.

THREE

FLY ME TO THE MOON

"Fly me to the moon, let me play among the stars, let me see what spring looks like on Jupiter and Mars. In other words, hold my hand. In other words, baby kiss me."

-Frank Sinatra

Two years after the Super Bowl, in July of 2001, Nate proposed to me at the Windows on the World restaurant at the top of the World Trade Center in New York. Before he proposed, he took my hand and said, "Every morning, I wake up feeling exhausted. Everything hurts. But today, for the first time in my life, I woke up, and I wasn't tired. Because today I knew I was going to ask you to be my wife. Life with you is what I want—you are the most amazing woman I know, and I can't wait to go on this adventure with you by my side."

I cried and said, "And?"

He opened the box, and it was exactly what I wanted, a simply beautiful solitaire diamond.

"Will you marry me, Kelsey?" he said. I hugged him and grabbed his chubby face and said, "Yes, I'll marry you! We are going to have an exceptional life!"

We kissed, and all the waiters and people sitting around us began to clap and cheer. We were so young—I was 23, and he was 25—and so in love.

After he proposed, we called all our friends in New York and met up at a club called the Pink Pussycat. I only have vague memories of that place, but I'm certain it wasn't the classiest joint. When the club closed around 1 a.m., we headed to McDonald's. A fight almost started while Nate and his friends waited in line for a Big Mac. That's when I knew it was time for that magical night to end.

Two months later, two planes would fly into the World Trade Center. On September 11, 2001, I watched as the place Nate asked me to marry him—and so many lives—collapsed to the ground.

After we were engaged, Nate would often say to me, "I can't believe we're really doing this!" A lot of people couldn't understand why we got married so young when we both had so much we wanted to accomplish. But we knew that being together wasn't going to keep us from our goals; it was going to make them better and more possible to achieve.

The plan before 9/11 was for me to stay in New York until our wedding the following July. Nate was living in Kansas City and playing for the Chiefs, and I was in my second year working as a fundraiser for Easter Seals New York. But after the attacks, Nate and I talked on the phone and decided it was time for me to leave the city—and for us to move in together. I packed up my stuff, rented a car and headed home to Florida to spend time with my family before moving my life to Kansas.

Ten months later, in July of 2002, Nate and I got married on a beach in Sarasota, Florida. We both agreed on how we wanted this weekend to go: close friends and family on a beach with a simple barefoot ceremony followed by a night of dancing and fun.

We started the fun part on Thursday night with a big, cheesy booze cruise. This was Nate's dream event; there was nothing that man loved more than beer and boats. He'd always had an obsession with boats. They were his happy place. Yet despite his passion, Nate had no idea how to drive a boat, didn't understand the tides and would often get caught up in the beauty of the ocean to the point that passengers were at risk.

Fortunately for our guests, we had a paid professional behind the wheel of this two-decker pontoon boat. As Jimmy Buffett played over the speakers, we set off into the Gulf of Mexico with everyone we loved, breathing in the salt air, drinking fruity cocktails and marveling at the setting sun. By the look on Nate's face, I knew he was in Heaven.

The next night was our rehearsal dinner—an intimate meal with just our families, followed by an evening with everyone at a beach house we had rented at the resort. Everyone we loved mingled and caught up with friends they hadn't seen in a while. People gave heartfelt toasts and a few inappropriate ones, but all of them made us laugh and cry. We went to bed that night feeling very grateful.

The day of the wedding started out rainy. There were big, dark clouds hovering over our wedding location on the beach. For some reason, I wasn't worried about the storm—which was unlike me.

"If we get married alone in the rain, that's fine with me," I said. "We can just meet up with everyone at the reception. So be it."

I found Nate walking alone on the beach and stopped to give him a hug. He looked nervous. "You okay?" I asked. He looked at me with his kind eyes and said, "I'm okay, just processing it all." I laughed because I knew he never dreamed of getting married at this age and also that he was marrying me. That would give any man pause!

Later in the afternoon, we were about to move the ceremony inside when suddenly the skies opened, and the clouds disappeared. From that point on, the whole day was perfect. Yes, the wind was blowing so hard you could barely see, and the microphone didn't work during the vows and we were short about 20 chairs. And of course our photographer passed out before the reception, a few friends slept on the beach after being over-served and there was a tiny bit of family drama since both of our parents were separated or divorced. But other than that, it was ideal.

The reception was everything we wanted, but "picture perfect" or "classy" is not the way I would describe it. The DJ played old-school hip hop, there was *one* Bird of Paradise flower on every table and the dinner was a buffet style pasta bar. If you were looking for a fancy wedding hosted by a Super Bowl champion, you were in the wrong place. But if you were looking for a good time, we had you covered.

Nate wasn't very concerned about the wedding details—except for one. He wanted the party to be long and loud, and he never wanted anyone to wait for a drink. His buddies were traveling from Allentown and other places and spending money on hotel rooms and flights, so he felt the least he could do was make sure they always had a drink in hand. When we were finalizing everything with the resort, he requested one unique setup: along with the two open bars and passed cocktails, he wanted there to be four kegs strategically placed behind fake trees in the corner of the reception area so his buddies would never have to wait.

People danced, ate and enjoyed every minute of that night. The biggest surprise was toward the end of the reception when Nate got up to give a speech. He thanked everyone for coming and then turned to me and said, "I have loved you since the first day we met, and you are the most beautiful, smartest, and talented woman in the world."

After everyone clapped and dried their eyes, he looked over and nodded at the DJ. No one was sure what was happening as he slowly began to serenade me with "Fly Me to the Moon" by Frank Sinatra. It brought the crowd to their feet. At 6'5 and 300 pounds, he danced and pranced and twirled with undeniable commitment. His performance was off-key but filled with passion and love.

I just stood there and took it all in with a big smile on my face. As the song went on, and especially when he hit some dicey notes, I laughed and looked around, feeling so grateful that my friends and family were witnessing what I had known all along: this man was the best. I was so proud he had chosen me.

After the reception was over, Nate and I headed up to our room. We sat on our balcony and looked out on the Gulf of Mexico. We saw some of our overserved friends stumbling around the beach and attempting to skinny dip with people they had met on the dance floor. The kegs were drained, the vows had been shared and Nate patted the bed and asked me to sit down.

Suddenly he got very serious. "Kelsey," he said. "I would really like you to take my name. I want us to have the same one."

Maybe it was the booze or the exhaustion or the wildly unappealing sound of Kelsey Durkin Hobgood Chittick, but I started laughing.

"Kelsey Durkin Hobgood Chittick," I snorted, collapsing onto the bed in laughter. Nate looked a little hurt but also amused. Finally, I was able to breathe. I liked my name, and I was comfortable with who I was. I felt like Kelsey Durkin was going places. We agreed to table this discussion and talk about it again at a later time.

At some point during our honeymoon, which mostly included us driving from The Keys to the Panhandle and staying in less than desirable locations, he brought it up again.

Because love makes us do crazy things, that week I said to him, "You know, I'd be okay with Kelsey Durkin Chittick."

A few months after our wedding, we were living in Kansas City, waiting to see what NFL team Nate would play for next. Nate's entire career had been spent going from team to team; he was what they called a journeyman. He played on seven teams in six years, and he loved it and hated it at the same time.

Football undeniably filled Nate's life with so many blessings. There's no way he would have gotten into UNC without the help of football; he just wasn't academically strong enough. And if he hadn't gone to UNC, we never would have met, and that is a *big* deal. That means we wouldn't have fallen in love, gotten married or had our kids. Through football and all his different teams, we met wonderful people, lived in great places and had amazing experiences. Many of the best men I have ever known were high school, college or pro football players. These men are huge, and so are their hearts.

During that time, when we were newlyweds and waiting for the next team, we took a trip out to Manhattan Beach, California. We stayed with his best friend and old UNC roommate Chris Keldorf and quickly fell in love with the West Coast lifestyle. We needed a home base, so after flipping a coin (heads, Carolina; tails, California, like the country song), we chose California. Our three-week visit turned into 19 years, and California is still the place I call home.

Only a few months after we moved to LA, Nate got picked up again by the St. Louis Rams. I stayed in LA and started working for Johnson & Johnson in their outside sales department. Nate's stay in St. Louis was short, and after being released, he was picked up by his final team, the Arizona Cardinals, just in time for training camp. As Nate headed off for camp, he confided in me how he felt about football.

"I am going to give it one more try, but I am tired, and my body is killing me," he said. "I don't know how much longer I can do this." It turned out that, as fate would have it, when the final cuts were made, Nate didn't make the Cardinals roster.

He called me from his hotel room and said, "Well babe, it's over, I'm done. I'm sad, but I am also very relieved. Can you fly out here, help me pack up and then drive with me back to LA?"

When I got to Arizona, he looked so tired. For years he had suffered from heartburn every night. Eventually he had to sleep upright to avoid the pain. A doctor had told him that all the Vioxx and Advil he had taken over the years had eaten away at the lining of his esophagus and weakened his ability to keep food from coming back up. His back was on fire after just a short amount of time in the car, and his sleep apnea was something he worried about every day.

"Honey, don't joke," he would tell me when I made fun of the mask. "You know I could die from this."

All of these ailments were related in one way or another to his time on the field—the repetitive hits and falls and blows that he endured over the years. He was constantly in pain even though he tried his best not to show it. Even if he wasn't completely ready for football to be over, his body was done playing.

On the ride back, we began to talk about what would be next for him and what jobs he might be interested in. He literally had no idea where to start. For the previous six years, football was all he focused on, and now he needed a new career. The problem was he didn't have a resume, didn't know anything about emailing or computers and was overwhelmed by the transition into this new phase.

As Nate looked out the window, he said to me, "Kels,

I want to help people, but I have no idea how to make that a job."

A few minutes later he looked at me. "What about social work?" he asked.

I told him it was an admirable career, but financially it would be an adjustment. It felt like he would be making a 180-degree shift from what he had just been doing, and we were both a little scared. I joked, "If you want to help people with drinking and drug problems, just keep playing football--think of all the people you could help on your team!"

We discussed how football is about dominance, masculinity and winning. Social work is about solutions, community and serving people. I kept wondering if there was something else he might love, but we couldn't come up with anything.

The transition from football into the real world is a big adjustment, and many guys struggle during this time. We both knew he just needed to keep moving and social work sounded like a good choice for now. He had come from a family that valued service, and his love for helping people ran deep. There was something about the way he listened and cared that truly lifted people up, including me.

In many ways, social work would be ideal for Nate because he was so present, gentle and kind; he reminded me of my granddaddy. My grandfather, Hiram Archie Clegg, was the greatest man I have ever met. He was ahead of his time spiritually, well-read and the most loving man I have ever known. Both men had a deep desire to serve, learn from and listen to everyone. They both had a way of making you feel like you were the most important person in the world. They rarely complained and deeply valued their time with their family. When Nate used to get home from work, I would ask, "How was your day?" And he would always respond, "Phenomenal...and now comes the best part!"

So on that car ride home from Phoenix, we decided that because I was doing well as a pharmaceutical sales representative in LA, my job could cover our bills and rent while he went back to school for two years to get his master's in social work. The plan was to be on a tight budget and use the savings from football for a down payment on a house.

After he finished some prerequisites at El Camino Community College, Nate was accepted into Cal State Long Beach's Master of Social Work program. But I was worried because school had always been a challenge for him. For most of his life, he thought he was stupid because he didn't read well until middle school, and he struggled with standardized tests. Before he began his master's, I encouraged him to get tested for a learning disability. He was embarrassed, but I convinced him it could help.

A few weeks later, he came home after being assessed at the college, and he was absolutely elated.

"Baby, baby, where are you?!" he yelled.

I came into the living room, and he showed me the results. "I'm smart! I'm not stupid! Can you believe it?!"

I gave him a huge hug. "Turns out I just don't process things quickly," he explained. "If I can take a test without being timed, I can do so much better!"

I could feel his relief. All his life he had thought he was dumb, but now he understood that he was severely dyslexic. It interfered with his processing ability, but he was also very bright. He had felt alone for so long. Now he had support.

From then on, he took all his tests without being timed, and that small adjustment made all the difference. He graduated valedictorian of his class.

While he was working on re-entering the real world, I happily sold my soul to the pharmaceutical industry. I was like a UPS driver with an entertainment budget—I spent my days dropping samples of heartburn medicine off at doctors' offices, taking people out to lunch and dinner and then driving my company car to the beach. It was a dream. Even though it took very little mental capacity and didn't fill my soul on any level, I enjoyed that job and everyone I worked with during those years.

After about two years of marriage, I sat Nate down, handed him a cold beer and said, "I think we should get pregnant."

His whole face drained of color. "Wait, what? Kids!" he said. "We just got married! You're 26, and I'm only 28."

I was prepared for this response. "All true but something in me says the time is right," I responded. "I can feeeeel it in my soul."

He shook his head and said, "Listen, Ms. Feeler, I don't get why we have to rush. Our lives are going so well!"

I knew he wanted kids eventually--in about six years. I grabbed his hands and said, "Trust me on this one; we are ready. It's time. We'll be young parents, and you'll have time with the baby and can help me when I'm at work. You can do schoolwork at night, which works best for you anyway. It's a perfect situation."

Two more beers, along with my persistent argument got him to relent. With a seductive look, he said to me, "Well, let's get to work."

Luckily we got pregnant with Jack right away, and Nate was thrilled when he found out it was a boy.

"Jack is his name!" he screamed the minute we saw the sonogram. He cried every time we went to an appointment and sobbed the minute Jack was born.

When we first brought Jack home from the hospital, Nate walked around the house holding him like Simba in *The Lion King*, saying, "You are the most amazing child ever to be born. You can live with us as long as you need but try to head out after 18 years."

He showed Jack every nook and cranny of the house and slept with Jack on his chest while he watched football on Sundays or the Yankees during the fall. When Jack was sleeping in his bassinet, Nate would lean over with tears in his eyes and say, "Can you believe we made that? How did we get so lucky? I had no idea I could love something so much."

When Jack was almost two, I brought up the idea of having another one. I wanted the kids to be close in age, like my brother and me, but Nate thought I was crazy. "Lady, we just had him," he said. "I need a break. That pregnancy and delivery were so hard for me!"

I resisted the urge to punch him in the face.

Jack's birth had been a traumatic delivery, and although Nate had been right there by my side, I also remembered a few times when he was watching me labor while sitting comfortably in a chair, eating a Philly cheese steak from the hospital cafeteria. I know it was hard for him to watch, but my compassion for him was fairly low —like zero.

I took his hands and said, "Buddy, trust me, it's time we have another one. The time is right, and I got the hard part."

So with very little resistance, we headed off for a quick vacation weekend in Florida, and before we knew it, we were pregnant again. Nate was certain it was a boy, but I knew in my gut it was a girl. No one in the family could remember the last time a girl Chittick had been born. It had been at least four generations, and when we saw her on the sonogram, Nate choked up. "I hope she is just like you," he said while holding my hand and crying.

When she was born five months later, he held her in a different way than Jack—more tentatively—and spoke to her in a quieter tone. From the moment she was born, all Nate wanted was to be her hero. He was as present and engaged as any father could be with his kids. Marriage and fatherhood were working for Nate, and he enjoyed it in an all-encompassing way. After we put them to bed each night, he would look at me and then lift his face up to the sky and say, "Thank you God for these kids. *This* is what life is all about."

FOUR
TRUTH & VASECTOMIES

"Marriage lets you annoy one special person for the rest of your life."

-Unknown

If you asked anyone about our marriage, they would say I was the bossy one. People thought I made all the decisions around the kids and was always telling Nate what to do. And that is *almost* completely true. It's also something I am working on feverishly in counseling. I feel like I am moving in the right direction, but I have a ton of work to do.

Let me begin by clarifying (defending) a few things. I was the boss about all the little items—like groceries, water bills and clothing. That was because Nate simply didn't care about them. But he did care *deeply* about a few big things. If he was passionate about something, he was the boss. Here are the areas where he had the final say: how we spoke to the kids, sitting down for dinner together, saying prayers, being a good teammate, looking people in the eye when speaking to them, limiting technology and serving people.

He also had strong opinions about how to invest our money (sometimes he was right, sometimes way off), what house we should buy (a great decision even if the inspector said, "I wouldn't buy this shit hole") and which team to bet on in football. All those decisions were in his "wheelhouse." Everything related to our day-to-day life was handled by me. And he was very happy with that setup. I'd say I was in charge of 90 percent of our daily life. As I write this, I can hear him screaming at me from Heaven that it was closer to 60/40, but since he chose to leave early and isn't here to defend himself, we'll say 90/10.

The irony of me doing most tasks is that when he died, much of my life remained the same. All those years spent taking care of everything turned out to be a great blessing. There were days when I thought, "I have more energy now than I did when he was alive." I think many women can relate because you are no longer wasting energy being mad at them or annoyed that they aren't helping more.

On some level, not having a choice helped; if something needed to be done, I had to do it. He wasn't going to take out the trash, help with the dishes, go to the grocery store or do any of the thousands of tasks that need to be done every day in the life of a family. I used to spend so much energy wishing he could or would help more. But then, since he was busy being dead, I knew I either had to take out the trash, have a kid do it or let it sit there. I finally understood that it wasn't the trash that was bothering me; it was that I thought *he* should be taking care of it. Now I take out the trash, and I'm not resentful anymore.

All of this has been an enlightening experience—it's made me realize that changing your perspective changes everything. Instead of keeping score or deciding what I thought someone "should" do, I realized it was my desire to change *him* that was causing the pain. I only wish I could have had this insight while Nate was alive.

Nate was a man who lived his life in compartments. He loved going to work in the morning, and he loved coming home at night. But in between, he never multitasked or lived between two worlds. At work, he checked out as a father; at home, he checked out of his job. This is a skill that many working men have but few working mothers experience. We juggle back and forth between realities and demands, barely making it on both sides. For us to unplug from either our kids or our jobs seems irresponsible to most of us.

So, by the time Addison was born and Jack was three, I had hit my limit. Two kids—a boy and a girl—were all I could handle. I had always worked and had just begun traveling back to the East Coast every few months for my company. It was clear I had nothing more to give. But Nate loved his life and loved being a dad. And since he was only "on" in the evenings, he thought having more kids might be a good idea. About a year after Addison was born, he asked about a third kid. He didn't know if he wanted us to have another biological child or if we should adopt.

I watched him as we had this conversation and just laughed. Of course he wanted another kid! I might have also if it didn't have to live in my uterus, come from my vagina, or drink from my boobs. Even if we adopted a child, *I* knew who would be the one waking up in the middle of the night, potty-training, figuring out childcare, and running the day-to-day details.

There were a few consistent conversations Nate and I had after each baby that made me certain that stopping at two kids was the right decision.

Kelsey: Delivering that baby was so hard.
Nate: I get it. Watching you in labor is so painful for me.

Kelsey: I am so tired that I could cry.
Nate: What are you talking about? The baby slept all night.
Kelsey: Um, nope. You did.

Kelsey: I hear her; she's awake. I'm going to feed her.
Nate: Is there any way you could breastfeed in the other room? I'm trying to sleep.

I didn't want more kids, but I could feel his desire to expand our family. Nate had a way of talking me into things, so I knew I needed to end this quickly. I decided to wait until he had a weak moment or did something that annoyed me. When these incidents inevitably happened, he would normally apologize and say something like, "I'm so sorry—I know how hard you work and how much you do for the kids and me. All you need is a little help."

The moment rolled around with the corresponding apology. And in that moment, I came in for the kill. "Nate, you are getting a vasectomy," I told him firmly. "We are done having kids. We have a healthy boy and girl, and I'm done. We are done. My privates can't take any more deliveries, and my soul can't raise any more children." He wasn't happy, but he knew he wasn't in a place to argue and that soon he would be under the knife.

For years, we couldn't even say the word "vasectomy" in our house because he would become so visibly uncomfortable. It was strange to see him so scared because, in general, he was a pretty tough guy. Sure, his favorite movies were *Patch Adams* and *Mr. Holland's Opus,* but this vasectomy thing had him all worked up.

Believe me, I understand that having someone cut your privates isn't fun. The 42 stitches I had after my son's birth aren't exactly a warm memory. But someone needed to make sure I didn't get pregnant again and that someone needed to be my husband.

We both knew it was time. We were in the honeymoon phase of parenting. Both of our kids could use a toilet, pour a bowl of cereal and sleep in a regular bed. They communicated clearly, happily went to school and thought we were great. They were old enough to know that we liked to sleep in on the weekends but young enough not to know anything about sex or drugs. We were clearly in the midst of the Chittick family glory days. Why ruin perfection?

Nate and I said a prayer for his vas deferens, said goodbye to our days as a fertile couple and made the appointment.

That Friday morning, I met my husband at home about two hours before the procedure. When I arrived, I found him sitting on a stool in the backyard. He was scared and sweating and shaving his privates. Outside. In broad daylight. Our neighbors have children and a deck that looks into our backyard. I knew we were in trouble.

Me: Are you okay?
Husband: Not at all.
Me: Can I help?
Husband: There is nothing anyone can do.
Me: What are you most worried about?
Husband: My balls.
Me: It will go quickly.
Husband: I don't want to do this.
Me: I know.
Husband: I am really scared.
Me: I know. Now, that's enough.

I was struggling to have compassion. He was going in for a 30-minute outpatient procedure but acting as if they were removing a limb. It took everything in my power not to remind him that during *both* of my childbirth experiences, I had been certain I was going to die. I was poked, prodded and pulled so much that I still struggle to talk about it. Both children got stuck in the birth canal, and they basically had to pull them out with a plunger. I had so many people with their hands in my business that when the janitor came in to clean my room, I fully expected him to lay down his mop, put on a glove and check to see if I was dilated.

I wanted to care that my husband was scared and nervous, but for some reason, it just wasn't happening.

During his consultation, Nate's anxiety was so extreme that the urologist had insisted that he take a Valium prior to the procedure. The problem was that my husband didn't take drugs. They made him nervous. He didn't smoke pot, he had never done mushrooms and he often claimed that Sudafed and Mucinex made him hallucinate. (Shoot me.)

When we got into the car, he carefully swallowed the Valium and looked at me with a serious expression.

"How long until I feel it?" he asked forlornly. "Oh, God, my heart is racing."

I tried to get him to relax, to talk about normal things, but nothing was working.

Eventually the drug started to take effect, but the result was less than ideal. He seemed very far away and still extremely anxious. As we pulled into the parking garage, he began whispering to himself like a crazy person: "You can do this! Don't be afraid! You are strong! You got this one!" It was uncomfortable to witness, but I did my best to be supportive.

During his 30-*minute* surgery, I sat in the waiting room. I wish I could say I hurt because he was hurting or that his pain was my pain, but that would be a lie. While he was under the knife, I found myself reveling in the silence and peace of the empty waiting room. It had been so long since I had been alone in a room with nothing to do and no one around me that it felt like a mini-vacation! I read a bunch of magazines from 2010, caught up on some emails and ate a Snickers bar. To be honest, I had a lovely time.

A half hour later, the doctor came out and said that all had gone well and that my husband would be out soon. As I looked up, there was my sweet husband, slowly walking towards me. He looked horrible. He was white, shaky, and appeared to have aged 10 years. This is the conversation we had:

(While reading the dialogue below, please picture a big blond man with a low, deep voice who is speaking very slowly while sweating profusely from his forehead.)

Me: How did it go?
Husband: It was horrible. The worst thing I have ever gone through.

Me: Oh, honey, it only lasted 10 minutes, and now you are done.
Husband: I wanted to die—I felt so violated. I prayed for it to be over the whole time.
Me: Don't you think that's a little dramatic?
Husband: Not at all! You have no idea. There was smoke coming from my balls.
Me: Honey, I had two kids. They were eight pounds each and left me with 42 stitches. But you are right, the smoke thing would be strange.
Husband: I am so glad it is over. It was awful. Oh, I was so scared!
Me (giving husband side hug while thinking to myself, "What a baby!"): I am so proud of you.

Then the doctor came back and explained the procedure and what we needed to do next.

Husband: So, doc, you cut into my balls and snipped the thingy that the sperm traveled in?
Urologist: Yes, I made an incision into your testicles and cut the vas deferens.
Me: So, his balls are going to be swollen for a while, and there is no way we can do it for at least a month, right?
Urologist: Yes, his gonads will be slightly enlarged for a period of time, and it would be best to abstain from intercourse until he heals.
Me: So, I don't have to do it for a while?

Husband: He didn't say that.
Urologist (visibly uncomfortable): That's something you two can work out later.
Me: But we should give that area a break, right?
Urologist (more visibly uncomfortable): Again, it is up to you how you want to move forward.
Husband: How soon can we do it again?

At this point, the doctor realized this conversation was going nowhere and quickly excused himself.

For three straight days after the procedure, I woke up next to a very large man with a bag of frozen peas on his privates. I did my best to take care of him, but I am pretty sure I won't be winning any awards. I tried to understand that what he experienced was traumatic, but on some level, I was just not buying it. After having my kids, I know I didn't come home and spend the entire weekend watching football, drinking beers and lying on the couch, hanging out with my friends. If I remember correctly, I was woken up every two hours by a small newborn who would gnaw at my breast, scream in my ear and poop all over me. When my poor, maimed husband said he couldn't stand up and asked if I would mind bringing him his breakfast in bed, it took all I had not to lunge at his throat.

FIVE
SAYING GOODBYE

"'Tis better to have loved and lost than never to have loved at all."

– Alfred Lord Tennyson

It was the fall of 2015, two years before Nate's death. We lived in a quintessential Pleasantville town where the kids walked to school, the neighbors watched out for each other and the high school football games were the place to be on Friday nights. Our kids were the perfect ages: seven and 10. It was the glory days of parenting. In some sense, we had made it. It should have been the happiest time of my life.

Although we had been through some very difficult financial times (it's mandatory for NFL players to make bad investments and lose money at some point in their careers), those events were behind us, and we could finally breathe again. And when it came to our marriage, we were in love.

Like many couples, we found that starting new careers and raising young children was challenging. There were rough days, months and years. But by the grace of God and a lot of honest conversations, we had made it back to deeply connecting again. We loved hanging out on the weekends and working out together in the mornings. We enjoyed each other the way people do who have been through ups and downs and built lives together.

Yet during this time, my anxiety level was super high I couldn't get out of my head. Every day during my walk, I would think, "Something is off; what is wrong with me? I can't figure out why I'm so anxious. Is it the kids or Nate or my job? Does everyone have this sense of foreboding that keeps them up at night?" I was riddled with stress, and I literally thought I was going crazy.

For the previous few years, I had been working for a recruiting firm based in Raleigh, North Carolina. I loved our work and what we were building, but there was a lot of travel involved. As time went on, the travel started triggering my anxiety. I was nervous about leaving my family, but I had no idea why.

While I traveled quite a bit, Nate stayed home, building his career as a financial advisor. After a few years in social work, he had decided to make a career change. He'd always been interested in investing and the stock market, so he transitioned into the new field. He loved helping his clients save for retirement and invest the money they worked so hard to earn.

On the surface, our life looked like it was humming along. But underneath, I could feel something shifting. My gut, my anxiety and my heart were telling me to pay attention. I felt alert and out of sorts during this time. Nate seemed happy but tired. He worked hard, stayed present with the kids, but also seemed far away at times. I couldn't put into words what was bothering me, but I felt something hard was on the horizon.

I GREW up in Winter Park, Florida, which is a beautiful town near Orlando filled with gorgeous lakes and quaint cobblestone streets. Growing up there was magical--but thinking outside the box, especially when it came to religion, was not encouraged. Almost everyone I knew was a Christian except for my best friend Michelle, who was Jewish. In my house, conversations about religion were a little different than they were in the rest of our community. My family was very open-minded about religion and avoided labeling themselves as one thing or another. At dinner, we were always talking about God, the universe, the different types of faith and how we each have the power within us to create the life we want.

The summer before 10th grade, my parents told my brother and me that they were separating. Neither of us had seen it coming, so I was understandably surprised and sad. After my dad moved out, I threw myself into my swimming career, my brother started partying, and my mom turned her focus to studying personal growth. She was ahead of her time; she spent her nights and weekends listening to Joe Dispenza, doing tai chi and energy work, and studying the Enneagram way before it was mainstream. I learned a lot from listening to her.

But my true spiritual guide was my grandfather. Born in Georgia, he had always dreamed of seeing the world. He spent his life traveling, learning new languages, and educating himself on different religions. He often spoke about the power of our minds and taught us the importance of visualization, the gift of gratitude, and the power of co-creation. He said love was the only thing that mattered and reminded us to choose our words carefully.

He taught me to attend to my spiritual life, so when Nate and I moved to LA, we sought out a comfortable and inspiring spiritual home. We both found it in the Agape International Spiritual Center, a transdenominational congregation founded in the 1980s by Reverend Michael Beckwith (best known as one of the featured spiritual leaders in the movie *The Secret*). He would always share powerful insights and perspectives, reminding us that love is always the answer. As a result, Agape attracted a diverse community of thoughtful people who wanted to serve each other and live a joyful life.

From the time Nate and I had met at UNC, we had been trying to create a full and rewarding life and encourage each other to be the best versions of ourselves. But in 2015, when the kids were 10 and seven and we were moving into our 40s, I realized Nate was crushing life, and I was—well—coasting. Nate was focused on changing the world every day while I was desperately trying to make sure nothing would change in my perfect, white-picket-fence life. I guess I figured he was doing enough service for both of us.

I was invested in "feeling good," while Nate believed in community, curiosity and service. His passion project was an after-school program he started in Watts (one of LA's most poverty-stricken neighborhoods). In contrast, I had put my dreams of writing and doing stand-up comedy on hold because I was too busy being comfortable. I spent my days organizing closets, judging people, raising my kids and slogging through my safe corporate job. My life was very easy and very comfortable, but I felt dead inside. And I was afraid of *everything*.

That's when Nate and I read *The Code of the Extraordinary Mind* by Vishen Lakhiani. It was as if I had been waiting for that book my entire life; it put into words exactly what I knew to be true but had forgotten throughout my life. I passed it along to everyone I knew, including fellow football player Tony Gonzalez, who was one of Nate's closest and most spiritual friends. Tony was so moved by it that he emailed the author to discuss the book. They ended up meeting in Europe, and through that connection, Vishen invited Tony and October (his wife and one of my best friends) to an event called A-Fest in Jamaica. Tony couldn't go because of his schedule, but they said October could bring two friends, and she invited me.

A-Fest is an event put on by Vishen's company, Mindvalley. It is, according to its organizers, "an event that gathers an extraordinary community of change makers and visionaries who are driven by epic ideas to impact the world—entrepreneurs, employees, artists, leaders, innovators, visionaries and more." I wanted to go, but my anxiety was high, and I had been struggling with an overwhelming sense of being adrift and "lost" for the past two years—a feeling that manifested the most when I was away from home.

I had also started waking up in the middle of the night screaming for Nate. I went to bed before him most nights, and he would normally stay up for a few hours and watch TV in the living room. But some nights, I would find myself waking up in a cold sweat, certain he was gone. In a panic, I would scream for him. He would rush in and say, "Sweetie, don't worry, I'm right here. You're okay, sweetie! I'm right here."

No one, including myself, could figure out where this anxiety was coming from. I felt like I was going insane. I had everything I wanted: a wonderful marriage, two amazing kids and a great career. What the hell was wrong with me?

About a month before A-Fest, I was still debating whether or not I should go. Nate and I were celebrating my best friend's birthday in Manhattan, and the second night in the hotel, I had the biggest panic attack of my life. I couldn't swallow or breathe, and my brain was looping on the idea of going to Jamaica. In the middle of the night, I texted my friends and said I couldn't go. I gave them a million reasons why it wouldn't work: it was too far, my kids needed me, the hotel didn't look right, and so on. Everyone was convinced I was losing my mind, especially my husband.

I sat awake in bed, trying to breathe. Nate propped himself up on one elbow, pulled off his sleep apnea mask, and said, "This has to stop. You need *deep* therapy! You are going on this trip—there's no way out. You need to find your purpose and passion, and you *must* stop being afraid. We will be *fine* at home! All is well. Now, go to sleep."

So on Wednesday, November 8, Nate woke up early and drove me to the airport. That was unusual because it was a super early morning flight, and even though we lived very close to the airport, the man liked to sleep. Typically, he would have encouraged me to grab an Uber. But on this day, he insisted that he take me himself.

When we got to departures, he looked at me and put his hands on my face. "Go have so much fun. Please enjoy every moment and learn everything you can. We will all be fine here. I love you." We hugged and kissed goodbye, and then I got on a plane and headed to Jamaica.

The three days I spent there were not only some of the greatest times in my life, but they also changed me. Every speaker, every person, every moment. We danced in the mud. We listened to Wim Hof, a Dutch extreme athlete known for withstanding freezing temperatures; Jim Kwik, one of the top brain coaches on memory and learning; and Steven Kotler, the bestselling author known for researching "flow state" and maximizing our potential.

All of it blew my mind. The people I met made me laugh and think and remember that there *are* people doing good *and* having great success. I was determined to come back a different person. Everything had shifted; in my gut, I knew my life would never be the same.

I wasn't worried about my job, my kids or my husband but instead, I was fully present and immersed in everything. On Saturday morning, I went to the beach for a swim before the final excursion. I floated in that gorgeous water and felt the Divine all around me. I felt like something had changed, and I couldn't wait to share it with Nate. I knew he would be thrilled too and that I was finally going to be able to take my life to the next level. For most of our lives together, his only concern had been that I wasn't using all the gifts I had been given.

At lunch that day, a group of us sat around talking about our life struggles and our ideas for the future.

When it was my turn to speak, I said, "I believe in everything that is being taught here, and I am in awe of it all. I am so grateful for my life, yet I struggle with my purpose and meaning. I'm embarrassed to say that I have the exact life I've dreamed of, but still, something is missing. I just hope something catastrophic doesn't have to happen to make me wake up and find my purpose and passion to use my gifts to change the world."

I will never, ever forget those sentences.

I hadn't brought my phone to many of the events because I didn't want the distraction. But right before we left for the boats, I grabbed it because I wanted to shoot some videos. As we were about to board the bus, I saw a few calls come in from numbers I didn't know, so I ignored them. Then my best friend Michelle called, and I still didn't answer. I figured we could talk once I was done snorkeling, smoking potent Jamaican weed and talking to new friends.

Then a text came in from Michelle's husband, Chris, who was also Nate's best friend. It read: "CALL US ASAP." When Michelle answered, her voice was calm.

"Hi, Kelsey," she greeted me. "Don't worry—everything is fine—but Nate fell while he was at the trampoline park with the kids and may have had a seizure. We don't have any details. He was alone with the kids, so we are going to get them now. The paramedics are taking him to the hospital to check him out, and your mom is meeting them there. Don't worry—go have fun."

I can't explain why or how, but I knew on some deep

level that there was no seizure, nothing was fine and my husband was dead.

After that, it all happened fast. I tried to call the hospital, but nobody answered; it turned out that my mom couldn't call me because she didn't have any cell reception at the ER. I kept using FaceTime to try to connect with my kids and reassure them that everything was okay, even though their dad had been taken away in an ambulance and I was 6,000 miles away. I knew I needed to get home as quickly as possible. But there was only one flight from Montego Bay back to the US, and it was leaving in 40 minutes. I was still in my bathing suit inside the hotel lobby. Time was not on my side.

And then life slowed down to mimic the timelessness that happens when a person is in "the flow." It was as if I were operating in another reality, one that didn't follow the laws of time or space. My girlfriends and I threw my clothes into a suitcase, and we jumped in a taxi and started racing toward the airport. About six minutes into the drive down a bumpy Jamaican road, my phone rang.

It was my mom. "Hello, sweetie," she said. "The doctor would like to speak with you."

She passed the phone to the doctor. I took a breath and stared at my friends. The connection was horrible, but the message was clear.

"I am so sorry," the doctor began. "We tried everything—we did CPR for 50 minutes. We could feel his soul trying to come back, but in the end, he didn't make it. He passed away from a massive heart attack."

I turned to October and Graci and said, "He's dead."

October's scream was so loud that it's burned into my memory forever.

On November 11, 2017, at 11 am, my seemingly healthy, incredibly gifted husband, lover of all people and father to our nine- and 12-year-old children, had died at the age of 42.

SIX

ANGELS & AIRPORTS

"All God's Angels come to us in disguise."
- James Russell Lowell

The summer before my trip to Jamaica, I had gotten into the habit of walking alone on the beach every Saturday morning. Barefoot in the sand, I would gaze at the ocean and ask God questions. And then I would pray—about my life, the kids and Nate.

I would also listen to music. There was one song on my playlist called "I Have This Hope" by Tenth Avenue North, and every single time it played, I cried. It touched me in a way I can't describe, particularly one line: *I want to trust that You are near, Trust Your grace can be seen in both triumph and tragedy.*

There was another song called "Closer to Love" by

Mat Kearney that I also loved. It's about a woman finding out the person she loves has died. There is a line in the chorus that says: "*I guess we are all one phone call from our knees.*"

On 11/11 at 11 am, I got mine.

Once we got to the airport, everything was a blur. As we ran through the terminal, October asked for my passport. I suddenly realized I didn't have it or my wallet. My other girlfriend Graci grabbed my hand, and we ran back, retracing our steps. October was trying to get a ticket, and we were trying to find my lost wallet. It was absolute chaos, and people watched us in disbelief. We ran out into the street—and there it was, laying on the ground, totally untouched. Jamaica is known for its beautiful beaches and four-star resorts, but also for its high crime rate. The chances that no one had picked up that wallet and ran were very slim.

As we started running back to the gate with my wallet and passport in hand, I had a brief insight; I realized I wasn't alone.

Angels were on my side.

When we got back to October, we heard the woman from the airlines say in a kind Jamaican accent, "I'm so sorry Sweetie, we can't open the door. Not possible." I thought I might pass out. October and Graci started begging her to try to do something. One of them ran to see if anyone else could help because we had no other options. This was the only plane left heading to the United States.

I have seen so many poor souls run full speed through the airport, get to their gate two minutes late and be told they need to take another flight. I have never seen anyone open the door after they finish boarding. It may be the one rule in the world that never gets broken. But on this day, one filled with miracles, something changed. One of the girls found this huge, kind Jamaican man who worked in the baggage area. She explained my story and begged him to help me. He looked into my eyes and calmly said, "Give me a moment" and went to talk to the crew. I don't know what he said, but I do know one thing; they opened the door.

I looked at these two women, who had just supported me during the worst moment of my life, and I was overcome with gratitude. I grabbed them both, hugged them and said, "I love you both forever. You have no idea what you just did for me. Thank you from the bottom of my heart. See you at home." After I boarded the plane, October and Graci sat on a bench, still in their wet bathing suits, and just cried.

As I slid into my seat, I went into full shock. I started throwing up into the little white bag and couldn't stop dry heaving. I had chills and felt like my body temperature was dropping. The whole thing felt surreal, like I was living both inside and outside my body. I couldn't stop shaking. I thought, "This must be what it feels like to go insane." I was all alone, and I had no idea how I was going to make it to LA.

As I was sitting there, crying and shaking, not one

single person spoke to me. The couple in my row looked over and then quickly put their headphones on. I think they were returning from their honeymoon and hoped to enjoy the last part of their vacation. The lady across the aisle pretended she didn't see me and just kept reading her magazine. And the flight attendant, who seemed unsure how to deal with me, finally stood next to me and quietly said, "Please buckle your seat belt." I don't think I would have talked to me either. The only thing worse than sitting next to a crying baby on a red-eye is leaving a vacation to find yourself seated next to an emotionally unstable woman who is sobbing and dry heaving. They probably thought I was hungover, had been dumped, or forgot to take a Xanax.

I sat alone, staring at the seat in front of me, and all I could feel was fear. I grabbed my phone; I needed a distraction. I wanted to listen to a song or a meditation, anything that would calm me down, but nothing worked. I couldn't get my breathing to even out. About 20 minutes into the flight, I heard the seatbelt sign turn off. Suddenly, I felt someone standing next to me. Then I felt a hand lightly touch my shoulder. I turned my head and saw a beautiful Jamaican woman. Slowly, she reached down and put her other hand on my forehead. She stood in the aisle of the plane, hands on me, and began to speak quietly to me.

"Baby girl, I don't know what you're going through," she whispered to me. "And I do not know what awaits you on the other side of this plane. But I want you to know right now that you are not alone. God is with you. I am with you, and there are people all over the world praying for you." I didn't understand what was happening, but slowly, I began to feel calmer.

"Now I want you to slow your breathing down baby girl, and I want you to think about how you're going to deal with whatever it is that is waiting for you," she said.

I started to lengthen my inhales and exhales, and my body began to slowly recalibrate. And then the woman added before walking back to her seat, "Baby girl, you are stronger than you think."

Once she was gone, I started to breathe normally. And a huge understanding crashed over me like a wave. At that moment, I realized I couldn't bring Nate back, but I could decide how I was going to deal with him leaving.

I spent the next nine hours, including one layover in Texas, getting very clear on how I wanted to feel in a few hours, in a week, in a year, and even 10 years from now. That night I decided that my kids had already lost one parent, and they were not going to lose another. When we landed, the airline, now aware of my situation, let me exit the plane first. Because of that, I never got to see that woman again. But I know that she was an Angel, sent from above, and that she changed the direction of my life forever.

Around midnight, I walked out of the Los Angeles airport and got into my mother's car. My mother-in-law was with her. It was the saddest car ride of my life. No one could speak, and even if we could have, there were no words to share. The devastation was palpable. They drove me to Michelle's house, where my kids had been waiting for me all day.

When I walked into their house, I knew that how I started this conversation would be important. I knew the words I chose would set the stage for how the kids would understand his death and that it would impact the rest of their lives. I felt broken, but I also felt a deep strength. I was ready for this moment because I knew what I needed to say and who I needed to be. Now it was time to be their mother.

I slowly woke them both up and asked Michelle and Chris to give us a moment alone. Then I sat down on the couch with my kids and hugged them for a few moments before beginning the hardest conversation of my life.

"I am so glad to be here with you," I said. "And I'm sorry it took me so long. I have to tell you something really hard. Your father is gone. He died today."

They both started to cry, and we held each other for a while. They were so young, but old enough to know what this meant. When I felt like I could go on, I continued. "Now I need to tell you three very important truths. Are you ready?"

They nodded.

"First, your father would never have left you, or me, if we weren't going to be okay," I said. "It wasn't his style. Do you understand me?"

They nodded.

"Next," I continued. "I need you to know that I am enough. I have no idea how to do this without him—no clue—but right now, I'm enough for both of you. I want you two to keep being nine and 12 years old because I'm going to figure this out, and we're gonna have a great life. Do you understand?"

They nodded.

"Lastly, this is important," I said. "You are not victims. You had the greatest man for a father that I've ever known. He was the kindest, sweetest, most loving and patient human, and for your entire lives, he focused all that energy on you. Some people don't get that for a day. Don't ever forget you are the lucky ones. Do you understand me?"

Then I looked at their small, scared faces, and I asked, "What do you need from me?" And at the exact same time, they both said, "Mom, if you're okay, we're okay."

So, starting that day, I did what every mother would try to do. I did my best to be okay. Some days it was easier than others, but it has always remained my North Star.

SEVEN
MORGUES & MIRACLES

"Grief is like the ocean; it comes on waves ebbing and flowing. Sometimes the water is calm, and sometimes it is overwhelming. All we can do is learn how to swim."

- Vicki Harrison

There is a lot about death that I wish I had known prior to this experience.

I wish I had known that when you hug someone, it could be the last time. I wish I had known a regular conversation with a loved one could be the last time you hear their voice. And I wish I had known that sometimes you have to say goodbye to a person you deeply love in a morgue. I had never seen or thought about a morgue until that day, and for good reason. The idea that I would have to walk into one—and see Nate there—made *me* feel like I was going to die.

The first night after Nate died was horrific. It felt like we were in a nightmare, but we couldn't wake up. After I told the kids he had died, we drove home and fell into my bed. By 4 am we had been wailing on and off for hours. It was primal and incredibly scary. The kids would wrap themselves around me one minute and be flailing and freaking out the next.

We were jittery and jumpy and vacillating between shock and utter devastation. It's hard to explain how it felt that night, but the overwhelming sensation was physical. It felt like being burned alive. We couldn't find a comfortable position; everything hurt, and there was no way to get relief. The mental anguish was surreal. Our brains couldn't understand what was happening, but our arms were desperate for his hugs, and our ears needed to hear his voice. It was like we were having a collective mental breakdown. The kids would scream, then whimper, then yell, then sleep. Nothing felt right, and it was dark, both in my room and in our hearts. That night was void of life, void of anything that resembled joy.

I have no idea how much we slept, but it couldn't have been more than a few hours. As the light began to come into the room, I looked at my sleeping children and wondered, "How the hell are we going to survive this?" I slid out of my room and dragged myself to my office to call the hospital and start the logistical process of death.

When someone dies, no one warns you about the

paperwork you have to do, the places you have to visit and the decisions you have to make. It is one of the hardest parts, and on many days, it brought me to my knees. This part of Nate dying was something I was not prepared for.

When I got up on Sunday morning, I crawled to my phone and called the social worker at Harbor UCLA. She had left me a message late the previous evening asking me to touch base with her as soon as possible. I felt like I was in a movie or floating above myself as I dialed.

The social worker, Donna, answered and extended her condolences. "Oh, that's too young, sweetie!" she said.

And then she explained what would happen next with his body. She told me that because Nate was healthy and had died suddenly in a public place, they had to rule out foul play. The hospital and the county were going to investigate his death and make sure he died of natural causes. These deaths were called "coroner's cases," which meant his body would travel from the UCLA hospital morgue to the Los Angeles Coroner's building. Once the autopsy was complete, they would release his body to a mortuary where he would eventually be cremated.

I kept having her repeat the instructions because nothing was computing in my brain. I felt blank, numb, and sad. Finally, I gave up and said, "Okay, send him to the LA location."

She paused and said, "Well, sweetie, not yet. I have

some good news. In the past, in a case like this, no one could see the body. But literally four days ago, the law changed, and now families can come say goodbye to their loved one in the morgue. Once you say goodbye, then they will send him on to the city."

All I could think was, "Does this woman think she is doing me a favor?" I couldn't comprehend what she was suggesting. There was no way I was going to say goodbye to Nate in a morgue.

Donna had a way about her that made you feel safe and loved. Even though she dealt with these matters all day, she made you feel special, as if helping you navigate this traumatic situation was her only job.

Before I spoke with Donna that day, I didn't think seeing Nate was even an option. I guess I assumed that his death was the end of me having access to him. And even if I had known, I was certain that wasn't something I would want to do. I had never seen a dead person, and I can't even watch crime shows on TV. I explained all this to Donna, but she refused to listen. When I told her I wasn't going to be able to go see him, she got really quiet, and then we had this conversation:

"Sweetie," she said. "You need to come say goodbye to your husband."

"No, I can't do that," I sobbed. "I can't do it."

"Yes, you can. You need to do this for him and for you. And for closure."

"No, I'm not going to do this."

"Kelsey, listen to me carefully," she said. "You owe it to your husband to say goodbye."

Sobbing louder, I said, "I can't do it. I'll die. I am so scared."

"You won't die—you are too strong. See you tomorrow at 10 am."

"I can't."

"See you tomorrow," she said.

I was frozen with fear. But somehow, Donna's conviction made me believe it was best to follow her advice. I didn't feel tough or brave, so I decided to pretend to act the part of a "strong widow"—as if I was in a movie. It was one of many moments when I would blindly decide to jump into a river of pain and let the current take me. I had no idea how I would get through it, but I trusted Donna and knew she must have insights that I didn't yet.

I DROVE to Harbor UCLA with my mom and Michelle. My mom's strength and courage are one of the greatest gifts of my life. On the day Nate died, she had driven alone to the hospital to see him, thinking he was either seriously dehydrated or had had a seizure. Neither the paramedics nor the hospital had been able to call us because the kids had his phone and wallet, so no one knew anything except that he was taken by ambulance to Harbor UCLA.

My mom was the one who talked to me on the phone

and tried to keep me calm while I was still in Jamaica. She sat alone in the windowless, beige waiting room without any information. They wouldn't disclose his death for hours because she wasn't listed as his next of kin. Eventually a nurse and a doctor walked in, and she knew the news was not good. After the ER doctor spoke with her, she asked if he could tell me over the phone. She called me from the back of the hospital, near the loading area where she could get service, and then handed her phone to him. She listened as he delivered the most devastating news of my life. And finally, she had had to hear me scream in pain when the doctor said, "I'm so sorry—Nate didn't make it...he passed away from a massive heart attack."

After we hung up, my mom waited for Nate's mom, brother and best friend to arrive at the hospital. Each one of them thought Nate was fine and would most likely be checked out by the afternoon. When she found them in the parking lot, all she could say was, "It's not good" and then tell them he was gone. Delivering that kind of news takes a level of strength and resolve that not many people have. I was so glad she was in charge at that moment.

Michelle had been by my side for the past 30 years and has been there for every moment since. Through many blessings, gifts, twists, turns, and possibly our own magical powers, we created lives three streets away from each other in the same town. She married Nate's best friend Chris and is the godmother of my kids. She was my maid of honor, and I was hers. The uniqueness and closeness of our lives and families could be another book. We were both raised with joy, love and support and had never experienced this level of pain.

On the day Nate died, his brother went to the trampoline park to get the kids. At that time, no one knew anything. He dropped them off at Michelle's so he could go to the hospital. During this time, Michelle called me and told me to try to enjoy my last day in Jamaica.

When I called her house an hour and a half later, my voice was far away. "Hi," I said. "Are the kids near you?"

"No, they're outside."

"He's dead."

"Who's dead?" She sounded panicked.

"Nate. He's dead. I told you. He died." I was numb with shock.

The last thing I said to her was, "Please, don't tell the kids. I will hopefully be home tonight."

So she was left staring at her nine- and 12-year-old godchildren, who had no idea they had just watched their father die. As she waited, the kids kept asking her how he was doing, and she had to lie. "I don't know," she told them, "but I think he is pretty sick."

She still feels guilty for lying to them, but I needed to be there to hold them when I told them he was gone. I will never know how much strength it took for her to hold in her own grief as she watched over my kids and waited for me, knowing that they would soon learn they no longer had their father.

My mom and Michelle were the two people I needed with me when I said goodbye to Nate.

WE PARKED, walked into the hospital and checked in. Like most people, I hate hospitals. They can be such sad and sterile places, and the smell of antiseptic makes me want to cry.

We went to the desk and asked for the morgue. Everyone was confused. They didn't know about the new law that allowed families to visit coroner cases. After speaking with Donna, they told me we could go in with a social worker, two police officers and a nurse. Donna arrived about five minutes later. She gave me a big hug and said they were ready for us.

With a nurse, the police officers and Donna, there were seven of us in the elevator. Michelle was hanging back, giving us space, and I remember Donna saying to her, "Get on up there, best friend."

The elevator ride was surreal. All I remember is a skinny, sick elderly man in a hospital robe and a sad, overweight couple who were all going somewhere they didn't want to go. The ride was silent; I was crying and wringing my hands. Like a movie scene, the elevator door slowly opened, and we began to walk down a long, cold hallway. I could see a door open on the right.

As I glanced into that room, I immediately saw Nate. He was on a gurney about a foot off the ground and had been pulled out of the bottom shelf. The morgue looked and felt like a very cold locker room. Sterile and bright, it was like a place on *CSI* or some murder show. There was a huge wall of lockers: five rows across, four down.

I thought I was going to pass out, so I leaned against the doorframe and closed my eyes. The last time I had seen Nate, I was kissing his sweet face as I said goodbye to him at the airport.

Michelle said, "You don't have to do this." I knew I didn't have to, but I also knew I needed to. I opened my eyes and walked over to Nate.

I stood above him, looking down at his face. "He looks exactly like he does when he's sleeping," was my first thought. He had a white sheet pulled up onto his chest, and the tube they used to intubate him was still in his mouth. His head was tilted toward us. I linked my arm in Michelle's and knelt down next to him.

I had a picture of Nate and the kids in my back pocket, but I never took it out—instead, I just started talking to him. In that moment, I felt so grateful to be with him again even though his soul was already gone. I was overwhelmed with love for him and the life we had built. I cried because I missed him so much, and I wanted to go back in time and change all of this. My heart felt like it was breaking, but immense gratitude kept showing up too. It didn't feel like this moment was real, so I asked the nurse, "Can I touch him? Can I touch his face?"

She quietly said, "Of course."

I slowly put my hands around his face, feeling his

beard, and said, "You're so stubbly." That was what Addison would say to him every night when he would give her goodnight kisses.

As I held his face, I climbed on top of him and thanked him for being such an amazing husband and father. "I love you so much," I told him. "We miss you so much, but I promise you, I will find a way to be okay." I put my head on his chest and whispered to him, "Go, sweetie, it's okay. Don't worry. I love you. You can go."

I sat up, rubbed his face one more time and stared at him, feeling all of our 21 years of memories, love and admiration. Then I gave him a last kiss and promised myself I would remember that moment in my mind forever.

When I was ready, I looked up at everyone and said, "I'm good." We all headed back into the elevator. As we were walking down the hall, I whispered to Michelle, "How do you think it went?" She looked at me with a small smile on her face. "Honestly, it was beautiful. And it reminded me of every conversation you two had when he was alive. You talked non-stop, and he just stared at you quietly and listened." We both laughed as tears poured down our faces.

As we entered the lobby, Donna stopped me and said, "You were so brave. And I want you to know that my maiden name is Addison." We hugged, and I thanked her for being an angel along my path.

Then we walked out of the cold, dark hospital into a bright, 72-degree, sunny Los Angeles day.

On the drive home, I was overcome by gratitude and shock. Gratitude that I got to see him and shock that he was dead. But what surprised me the most was that once I had gotten to see him and started talking, it wasn't as scary as I had imagined. And right then, driving my car after seeing my husband's dead body, I had a flash of insight: so many fears we have are just constructs in our mind. We can handle so much more than we think is possible.

The next day, the kids asked me what was going to happen to his body. I looked right at them and lied--again. The first time I had lied was before I flew home from Jamaica:

"Is Dad going to be okay?" Jack had asked me over FaceTime.

"He's really sick, and it doesn't look good," I lied to both of them, "but right now he's okay."

I couldn't bear to tell them the truth without being there. It was the best I could do. I knew some day in the future I would need to apologize for that, but it felt like the right decision at the time.

This was the second time that I couldn't find the courage or words to tell them the truth. That day, they made me promise that I would never burn his body. Frankly, none of us could bear the thought of him being cremated—it just felt too real and too scary to imagine his body going through that process. At that moment, I pretended it would never happen.

When the kids asked me where his body was, I told

them he was in downtown LA at a place where dead people stay.

"What happens if he comes back alive and then he's trapped in the coffin?" Jack asked.

Without missing a beat, I said, "Oh, sweetie, don't worry. They have speakers in the coffins. If Dad comes back, he'll just knock or say he needs help, and someone will come and get him out."

Not my best mothering move, but I just didn't know what else to say. For a while, that story gave them a lot of false peace and comfort, and I felt pretty proud of myself.

But then I shared what I had told them during my one-on-one with their therapist the following week.

"Wait, what did you say?" my therapist asked. "That he was in a hotel for *dead* people?"

"Pretty much, yes," I said. "A dead people hotel."

"Like a Hyatt for dead people?"

"Exactly...Was that the wrong choice?"

"Ummm, yes," she said. "We are going to need to discuss that one."

My children's therapist sternly explained to me that lying about death could cause the following reactions: confusion, lack of trust, false hope, and the idea that their father could come back to life (which most people agree won't happen).

I understood her point, but I had to say one quick thing before I left.

"I know no one really believes that you can come back from the dead, but I would like to point out that millions of people think that is exactly what Jesus did! Anyway, have a great day!"

I headed out to my car, understanding that someday soon, I would need to have an honest conversation with the kids.

But in the end, I would do it all the same way again. When you hear your children crying for hours and see the fear in their eyes as they imagine their father being cremated and gone forever, you will say any crazy thing you can think of to lessen their pain.

In my heart, I know Nate would have enjoyed his imaginary stay at the Hyatt for Dead People—he loved a good happy hour and having someone make his bed. These days, I don't beat myself up when I make a mistake, make a situation worse or say something I later regret. When you are going through hell, you do what you need to do. I just try to honor what feels right.

My hope is that over time, when there is less pain and more peace, I can apologize, tell the whole truth and rest in the idea that I was doing the best I could in an extremely hard situation. And that counts for something.

P.S. There *should* be a hotel for dead people. No one wants to be cremated or buried in the ground. It's time to think out of the box—literally.

EIGHT

MEMORIES & MEMORIALS

"To heal grief requires outside assistance. When we are bereaved, we need to be compassionate with ourselves as we seek out those who are willing to walk with us in our grief."

– Anonymous

It was 72 hours after losing Nate.

That morning I opened my eyes, and for a split second, I was certain it was all a dream. But then I rolled over to say good morning to Nate, and there was nothing but an empty, cold place.

"Holy shit, my husband is dead, Nate is gone and the kids don't have a dad!" I thought as the panic rose and the tears began to roll down my face.

Then I told myself, "Keep breathing, keep breathing...just get through the next five minutes."

After washing my face and putting on my robe, I slowly walked up the stairs. I wasn't sure what day it was or what I needed to do. I turned into my kitchen, and there were all 12 of my best girlfriends from high school. I didn't know how they heard the news, how they re-organized their lives or what they had to do to get to LA, but I didn't care. I was overwhelmed with gratitude. In that moment, my whole body relaxed, and I began to cry. I looked around and marveled at all the love and history I shared with these friends. I thought, "Over 30 years, 28 kids, 12 husbands, three ex-husbands and lots of Goldendoodles together." The women who had been with me on the happiest days of my life were now here to support me through the worst. They were in my house, and I didn't have to do this alone.

I looked around the kitchen table.

"Damn, I wish you all were here for a different reason!" I said. "Any chance I'm just living a bad dream, and this is really a surprise girls' weekend or a bachelorette for someone's second wedding?"

I wanted their presence to indicate anything but the fact that the love of my life had died.

That first week took a lot of energy. There were a few weird moments when I would look at all my friends and think, "How fun, all of my friends and family are here!" But by the time I exhaled, the truth of my situation would descend upon me, and I would fall back into the abyss.

I was beyond grateful and completely overwhelmed at the same time.

My brother Clegg had heard the news about Nate while at a party in Fort Lauderdale and had immediately taken an Uber to the Miami airport, hoping to intercept me en route from Jamaica and fly the rest of the way back to LA with me. Unfortunately, my flight connected in Texas, so I didn't get to see him until the next day.

When he and my dad walked into my house, Clegg just fell to his knees. Over the previous 21 years, he and Nate had developed a beautiful friendship—lots of deep sea fishing and deep conversation. When he hugged me, I could feel his pain and his worry for the kids and me. Both he and my dad smelled of airplane cocktails and sadness when they arrived. I knew it was going to be a tough week for everybody.

Weddings and funerals are stressful events to begin with, but when you throw in sudden death, international travel, divorced parents and strong personalities, it becomes an especially interesting couple of days. Nate and I each have divorced parents, and while both of our families have so much love, there is always a healthy dose of drama when everyone is gathered. My body felt like it was on overdrive. I couldn't find ways to settle, and I wasn't sure how to handle it all. Having all that love and support was magical, but the logistics and stress were hard to manage.

I struggled to make decisions about anything. "I have

no idea where everyone is going to stay," I cried to Michelle as I saw more people show up each day.

Michelle hugged me and whispered, "They are here because they love you, and you don't have to do anything. Everything is under control." That would be Michelle's mantra to me for a long time. She, more than anyone, took on an unbelievable responsibility after Nate died.

Michelle had a very challenging situation. Nate was important to so many people in her life, but each in different ways. He was my husband, her children's godfather and her husband's best friend. Everywhere she turned, someone was grieving him. Both of our families were broken, yet she was the one that stayed strong. She showed up for me in indescribable ways, putting her own feelings aside so she could focus completely on all of us. One day she may need a lot of therapy because of this, and I am certain she is going to send me the bill.

People were sleeping everywhere; in hotels, in my garage, at neighbors' houses, at friends' places and a few on my couch. Everywhere I looked, there were people waiting to help.

One morning I woke up and walked out to my living room. Disoriented as usual, I rubbed my eyes to make sure I wasn't crazy. There, laying on my couch, was Betsy, my roommate from New York with whom I had shared some of the best years of my life. I never dreamed she would show up because, although we adored each other, I hadn't seen her much over the last 15 years. Family and life had gotten in the way.

She heard me walk in and sat up. "Kelso—I'm so sorry," she said.

"Betso, I can't believe you came. What the hell happened to my life!?"

We hugged and cried. "Holy shit, I'm glad you're here!" I said. "I wish we were hungover, recovering from a wild night of dancing and French kissing strangers. Take me back!"

Betsy and I had been living together on September 11, 2001. "Besto," I asked her, "remember on 9/11, when we were both trying to get home after the towers had fallen?"

She nodded. Neither of us would ever forget that day.

As we talked about it, I could feel that same panic I had felt over 15 years ago. "Remember I was running through the park, heading back to the apartment, desperate to find you and our friends?" I asked her. The scene in the park was unreal. There was no public transportation, and everyone was on foot. The people walking north through the park looked like zombies—everyone was covered in soot and white debris.

It was one of the scariest days of my life, but I also remember feeling so much love and support.

"Remember how everyone was helping each other, giving people water or new clothes, donating blood and handing out food and shoes?" I asked, and she nodded. "There was so much pain and yet so much love."

That's how I felt the week after Nate died.

My doorbell rang constantly with a steady stream of caring neighbors. If you haven't visited our town, you are missing out. It's a special place. El Segundo feels more like a quaint midwestern town than a suburb of the 2nd largest metropolis in the United States. Kids play in the street, neighbors talk, the baseball field is packed with fans and there is a free shuttle that takes you to the beach.

It's not perfect, of course. It's located between LAX, an oil refinery and a water treatment plant. Erin Brockovich would have a field day. But we look the other way and trust the ocean winds are helping to keep the air clean because it's an amazingly supportive place to raise kids.

For an entire year after Nate died, my dear friend Anne, who lived on the other side of town, would ring the doorbell promptly at 8:30 am. "Here is your coffee," she would say. "Is there anything I can do to help?"

One day I confessed to two of my closest friends and neighbors, Chris and Troy, that I was scared to sleep in the house without Nate. The next morning there was a Ring security video doorbell on my porch. The attached note said, "You are always welcome to spend the night at our house."

The neighborhood kept delivering in every single way. There was food and flowers, water and cards. But there was also laundry detergent and candles, tampons and soap. The tampons were such a welcome surprise. It's bad enough to lose your husband and feel as if you're going through hell, but to also get your period at the same time and run out of tampons would just be cruel.

That week I wore a uniform: pajamas and a beautiful orange cashmere scarf. The scarf was a gift from my friend Ashley, who walked into my house, took a scarf off her neck and wrapped it around mine. As she looked into my eyes, she said, "This scarf will keep you warm; it saved me during the hardest year of my life." I had always admired her positive outlook and strength. That scarf stayed on me for weeks, reminding me I, too, would survive.

That week I learned that joy and laughter and sadness and tears are closely related to one another.

"Is this shit for real?" I would ask a friend each morning. By the sadness in their eyes, I knew it was.

"Why are you all so sad?" I would ask. "Did someone die?" We would laugh until we cried.

That week, I always had someone by my side. With arms linked, we moved from the kitchen to my bed to the sofa and often the floor. While staring at the ceiling, I would ask out loud, "How am I going to survive?"

And then someone would reply, "Because you are and have always been so strong."

It was an endless loop of "What the fuck am I going to do!?" followed by someone saying back, "You are doing the hard thing...you've got this, lady."

One day, someone texted to ask me about a date for the memorial. It had literally never crossed my mind. I was just taking it one minute at a time. A memorial was too overwhelming. People, flowers, speeches? I could barely sit up; how would I plan an event? Organizing my kids' birthday parties gave me anxiety and hives; planning a gathering after the sudden death of my favorite human sounded impossible. I told my father-in-law, "We aren't having one. I can't do it." He understood and didn't say anything else.

Luckily two of my very best friends, Lise and Karin, overheard that conversation. These two aren't normal friends or normal people. They are special, like fairies, and operate in a different sphere of life—one that produces the most magical parties, outfits and vacations. They were born to make life beautiful and bring people together. So, when they walked into my house, the energy immediately changed, and they took charge—of pretty much everything.

They sat down with me and said with a loving yet clear tone, "Kels, you are having a memorial. Okay, sweetie? We're doing something to honor him and you and the kids. People want to come celebrate Nate; we have it all under control." That was an understatement, to say the least.

In the next three days, Karin and Lise orchestrated the most beautiful Celebration of Life for over 400 people. While crying on my couch, I would hear one of them on the phone whispering, "Yes, we want a slide show...no, only white flowers... make it look really good...we don't have time, fix it!" Flowers, venues, music, slideshows and managing my family and Nate's. It was something to behold.

Meanwhile, I was crawling around my house in a bathrobe or sobbing on my couch. They didn't ask me one question, and that speaks to our deep 30 years of friendship and love. One day they decided Addison needed a new outfit. My friends thought I was a lot of great things, but fashionable was never one of them. My daughter deeply cared about her clothes, and they were not going to let her down; she would have a cute outfit for the memorial.

We headed to the mall, which was an odd outing but strangely comforting. Something about the escalator, the smell of Cinnabon and Claire's Boutique gave me peace. As Karin and Lise walked behind me, I heard them talking about the memorial. When I looked back, they suddenly got quiet and locked eyes. And then they high fived one another. It made me laugh so hard because whatever those fairies had decided, it had been done telepathically.

The memorial was perfect: beautiful flowers, 500 mini muffins and everyone we loved in one place. Every detail had been taken care of, and I had not made one single decision. For the worst day of my life, it turned out to be pretty spectacular, and that is because of their hard work and the people who showed up.

The only person missing was Nate. If he hadn't been dead, he would have loved it! I know he was watching from somewhere and thinking, "Finally! Took long enough to get all my people together. This is bullshit that I can't be there, but I love that everyone is talking about life, friends and family. Annoyed that it took me dying to make it happen, but this is *outstanding*!"

When Nate was alive, he loved to watch sports documentaries. Learning was his favorite pastime, and he couldn't get enough of inspiring stories about coaches and teams that accomplished great things. Whenever a show ended, Nate would turn off the TV and sit in the dark.

"Babe, the show is over...want to come to bed?" I would ask.

Inevitably, after a long pause, he would say, "Kels, have I done enough? Have I made a difference in this world?"

I would go sit on his lap and grab his face in my hands. "You have done so much, and you make a difference every day," I would say.

As I walked back to my room, I would look back at him still sitting there. It felt like on some level, no matter what I said, he didn't fully believe it.

Through the words of his friends and family, he would have finally known that he did what he set out to do: make the world a little better. It was a gift to hear so many stories about him, especially for my kids. They listened to every word and now knew all the people he had touched and loved along the way.

Once we knew there was going to be a memorial, Jack said he wanted to speak. At 12 years old, only days after he lost his dad, Jack stood up and gave a speech that changed our lives. He had never spoken in public before, yet he courageously stepped up to the mic. Nate had been an exceptional father, but it wasn't until Jack spoke that I saw clearly how much he had taught him.

"Hello everybody. As most of you know, I am Jack, Nate's son. Just to clear the air, if you are standing next to anyone you know or love, please give them a big hug. Just embrace.

My dad was the greatest influence on a growing 12-year-old boy. He always said, "The most important thing in the world is other people." You guys know the Emoji Movie, *right? One of the quotes that the main character said was, "What's the point of being number one if there are no other numbers?"*

That is what my dad was putting into me. He knew that I was able to be the caliber of a man to be the best version of myself. He taught me how to treat a woman. He taught me how to always give full focus whenever someone was trying to share something with me. And sooner, rather than later, those traits became habits. My dad made it seem like being above and beyond was regular. If I had a different dad that died, I probably wouldn't be speaking right now, you know? If I had a different dad, there might only be half as many people attending this memorial today. That's how many people he influenced through his actions. If I could have one more conversation with him, all I would do is just talk myself out of my skin. I would tell him everything I've always wanted to tell. And he would just sit there and look me straight in the eye.

And after I was done talking, he would rephrase everything I said into better form. He knew without even trying how to make me better. And that's how I want to remember him. Thank you.

There were moments along the way that gave me great hope, and Jack's speech was one of them.

As the memorial came to a close, Nate's best friend stood up. Chris was the reason Nate and I met, and then he had married Michelle. For 20 years, we had been blessed with a unique situation, our best friends married to each other. With the four of us and then our kids, we had everything we needed. We never took it for granted, and we knew life without Nate would never be the same.

Chris gave the last speech.

"Sometimes in life, if you're lucky, someone crosses your path that has an ability to see the very best in you when you can't see it yourself. This was Nate's greatest gift. This came so naturally to him. When you have the ability to see real goodness in someone or something and make that your focus, your ability to love and connect becomes very powerful.

We'll all miss him so much. I'll miss his deep and very loud belly laughs at some of the worst jokes you've ever heard. I'll miss his tears, and shoot, I'll even miss our heated arguments, especially around politics. Once Nate came over, and he rang the doorbell. I answered and asked, "What's up buddy?" Nate just stared at me and then said, "Chris, it's time for you to grow up!" I had no idea what he was going to say next. I mean, I'm married, I have a house and I have three kids. So I thought, "What could it be?" And then he said, "It's time to become a Democrat!" I laughed at him and jokingly said, "That's unacceptable. Now you have crossed the line!" Nate was furious, and we didn't speak for a week.

We all laughed hard at that. It felt great to have a physical release.

During the memorial, I felt like I was playing the part of "grieving widow." But once the day was over, I fell apart. I was exhausted. The memorial had made it seem real, and I wanted Nate to come home. On that night, I had nothing else to give. I just wanted it all to be over, so I excused myself and crawled into my bed. I had finally realized this wasn't a nightmare; it was my new life.

NINE
CORONERS & COFFEE

"So, it's true, when all is said and done, grief is the price we pay for love."
- E.A. Bucchianeri

About two weeks later, I woke up in a post Xanax haze. For the first time, I saw why people loved those pills, and also why you should try not to take them that often. As I opened my eyes after what felt like the best sleep of my life, it took me a minute to remember where I was and what had happened in my life. It scared me because it felt like the pill had taken me to a place of nothingness. Not that I didn't like it, but I was afraid I could get used to it. I hadn't slept for days and had been desperate for some rest so, at that moment, I was both very grateful and terrified of becoming dependent. The sleep had been so good that I was already craving the next night when I could take one. That feeling gave me pause. I knew that whatever I numbed out today would have to be dealt with tomorrow. There was no way around it.

As I rolled over and grabbed my phone, I made a mental note to stop taking these as soon as possible. My phone showed 36 unread texts, eight voicemails and 14 missed calls.

I got up, dragged my swollen face and foggy brain to the shower and tried to think about how I would survive this day. Once I got dressed, I journaled for a bit and then sat down to check my emails and voicemails. Most were from people sending me love and support, but there was one from an unknown caller.

"Hello Mrs. Chittick, this is Maria from the LA County Coroner." Her voice and demeanor sounded like someone who worked in a morgue, sad and lonely. "Your husband has arrived here, and we have his personal belongings. Please come down, check in at the front desk, get a parking pass and then wait in the lobby. When you are called back, have your identification and we will give you his wedding ring and wallet. Don't forget the parking pass, or you will get a ticket."

The day before, the hospital had told me that as soon as he was transported to the county morgue, they would contact me. At that point, they could either give me or mail me Nate's personal belongings. During that conversation, the woman had said, "I would recommend that you come down in person if you can. We have seen incidents where personal items get lost. Plus, to have them mailed, you have to fax some paperwork back." The thought of a mailman bringing me my husband's wedding band and wallet was unacceptable, and going to Kinko's to fax something sounded equivalent to running a marathon at this point. I thought it would be easier to run down there and get his things even though I dreaded stepping foot in a coroner's office.

I sat up, feeling numb. My processing time had gotten very slow, but two thoughts went through my head. The first was, "How the *fuck* does my plan for this day include going to a morgue to get Nate's ring?!" and the second one was, "I have to get a parking pass for the coroner's office? What type of place tickets people when they are picking up their dead loved one's belongings?"

There were thousands of hard moments that first month, but this was one of the worst. My aunt, who I call Tia, is like a second mother to me and bravely offered to go with me. "This is like the worst fucking field trip of my life," I said to her as we got in the car. We looked on the map and saw the coroner's office was located in the bowels of downtown LA. As we exited the freeway and were getting closer, we couldn't help looking at each other in disbelief of the situation.

If you have never been to the LA County Coroner, consider yourself lucky. It may possibly be one of the most depressing places on Earth. It is a sad, broken-down brick building completely devoid of hope. When you pull in, you can feel the energy turn dark. But the most disconcerting thing is how busy it is; it turns out that *a lot* of people die in LA every day. It's a very popular thing to do, and that is why parking is an issue.

Tia stayed in the car, as the aforementioned parking situation seemed very precarious, and I walked into the building alone. The lobby looked like a scene in a scary movie. Everyone who worked there looked half-dead, and the whole place smelled of formaldehyde. Families huddled together, weeping as they waited for their names to be called. The receptionist checked me in without ever looking at my face. Her voice was monotone as she stared down at her desk and said, "Your name will be called in 30 minutes. There are seven people ahead of you. Here is your parking ticket. You *must* put this in your car. Or you *will* get a ticket." And then: "There is coffee. Over there." She pointed (still without looking up) to the saddest coffee station I have ever seen.

I won't even get coffee while waiting for an oil change at Jiffy Lube. Why would I get coffee in a morgue on the worst day of my life? Life is sad enough, and the powdered creamer and small Styrofoam cups just reminded me it was only getting worse.

It all felt so gross and inhumane. It felt so—transactional.

I walked out to the car, handed Tia the super important parking permit and then I broke down. It all hit me at once, and I was overcome with devastation. It felt too big for me to handle, and I was struggling to breathe. I couldn't believe I was at the morgue, picking up my dead husband's belongings. Tia looked at me and her face mirrored mine, filled with sadness and disbelief. She rubbed my back as tears fell down her face, and she said, "It's too much, sweetie. I am so sorry. Somehow we will make it."

Without Tia, I would not have survived that day.

Eventually I received a text that it was our turn. Tia and I walked into the lobby and were directed to a small brown door. We took two steps inside before sitting down on tiny plastic chairs. In front of the chairs was a wall of clear plexiglass. A door behind the plexiglass opened, and a woman entered with a manilla envelope.

She unemotionally asked for my identification, reviewed it and then slid the envelope through an opening in the glass, all while looking at her phone. "Please open it, confirm the belongings and then sign next to the X on this paper." And then while still looking at the phone, she mumbled, "I'm sorry for your loss."

I opened the envelope and immediately felt sick. I poured his wedding band and wallet into my hands. I slid the ring onto my finger and looked up at the lady with tears in my eyes.

"Excuse me ma'am."

She looked up.

"He was the best. He was the love of my life. He died a few weeks ago on Saturday, in front of my kids. I miss him so much."

Something in her changed. She looked right at me and said, "I am so sorry to hear that. That is so hard."

I had a desperate need to make this personal because it all felt so unreal. After I signed the paper, I asked, "How long until the autopsy is complete?" She told me anywhere from four to six weeks, and a doctor would call me with the results.

I thanked her, and then Tia and I left the room. We walked through the lobby and out to the car without saying a word.

Days and weeks went by and no one called. I kept checking with the morgue, and they kept saying they were very busy. Until you have a dead person, you don't grasp the fact that so many people are dying each day.

As each week went by, I became more obsessed with knowing exactly why and how he had died. The longer it took, the more I felt like I was going insane.

TEN

HELMETS & HEARTACHES

Life presents many choices, the choices we make determine our future.

- Catherine Pulsifer

While I waited to hear back regarding the autopsy, I began to look through the paperwork the NFL provides to players and their families related to death or illness after they retire. The current conversation between the NFL and the Players Union is focused on benefits for possible long-term disabilities that many players face. I had heard the stories about the long-term effects football had on players' joints, hearts and bodies, but I was just beginning to read about the new focus on head injuries caused by the sport.

A few years before, I had seen a trailer for the movie

Concussion starring Will Smith. The movie focuses on Chronic Traumatic Encephalopathy or CTE, a brain condition associated with repeated blows to the head, and how it affects NFL players at a very high rate. The movie is based on the true story of Dr. Bennet Omalu (Will Smith), a forensic pathologist who conducts an autopsy on former NFL player Mike Webster (David Morse) and discovers neurological deterioration that is similar to Alzheimer's disease.

Maybe I was scared, or maybe watching a movie about retired football players with brain damage didn't sound fun, so I chose not to see it. I knew that during Nate's football career, he had taken thousands of hits to the head and body, and his time playing could have possibly contributed to his death. His autopsy would hopefully tell us what exactly caused his heart to fail, and I was very interested in understanding how playing foot ball may have affected his heart and his head. I wanted this information for my own peace of mind, but I truly needed it for my son. The results of this autopsy, and whether football could have contributed to Nate's early death, would determine if I ever let Jack play.

As we waited for the first autopsy report, Jack and I had a tough conversation.

"Jack, I'm sorry, but if anything in your dad's autopsy results indicates that his early death had anything to do with his time playing football, you will never play the game."

He didn't show much emotion, and I wasn't sure

what was going on inside his head.

"Mom, I understand. If football had any part in his death or any impact on his brain, I won't ever ask to play." I was grateful we were on the same page.

The coroner's office would be able to do a complete autopsy on his body and specifically his heart, but the test for CTE wasn't part of their protocol. CTE can only be diagnosed post-mortem, which means after the individual is dead. City coroner's offices don't typically look for this, and most don't have the equipment or expertise to diagnose it. I wanted to make sure we had the right doctors examining Nate's brain tissue for CTE.

Over the last five years, and especially the two years before he died, I had this nagging feeling that something was off with Nate. It's hard to explain, but he just seemed different at times. There were some business decisions he made that I firmly disagreed with and partnerships with people that I knew weren't good humans. In some ways, it felt like he had lost his typical discernment around people and began making riskier choices than I had previously known him to do. He also seemed to be getting sadder and more overwhelmed as the years went by, as if he were floating away from us. He wasn't as present, and he often seemed tired and confused. I wanted to know if that stress was from life, work and raising kids, or if there was something bigger causing it. My anxiety over the past few years, along with some of the changes I noticed in him, made me convinced I needed to find the best doctors and clinic to autopsy his brain.

After doing some research, I reached out to the team at Boston University led by Dr. Ann McKee. Dr. McKee is a renowned neurologist who heads up the clinical team at the CTE Center. There, she and her team conduct innovative research on Chronic Traumatic Encephalopathy and other long-term consequences of repetitive brain trauma in athletes and military personnel.

I was put in touch with Lisa McHale, who is the Director of Family Relations at the center. She is also the widow of Tom McHale, the second former NFL player diagnosed with Chronic Traumatic Encephalopathy. McHale was a lineman from 1987 to1995 and died at the age of 45 from an overdose after years of depression and prescription drug use linked to his CTE.

Lisa and her staff, along with the help of the LA county morgue, transported Nate's brain tissue to Boston University. The study would take approximately a year, and during that time, they would analyze both clinical and pathological data to determine if Nate had CTE. Once his samples arrived and they confirmed everything was set, I tried to put it out of my mind. I was hoping that when I spoke to them a year later, we would find out his brain was just fine.

When Nate was alive, I thought he was one of the healthiest guys I knew. He ate salads, he worked out and he was always telling the guys in the neighborhood to stay in shape, drink protein shakes and take care of their bodies. I never once thought he might have heart disease or a brain injury; it certainly never crossed my mind that he might die of heart failure at 42. Nate kept up with all his doctor appointments, with his own physician and trainer and also through the NFL's program.

A year before he died, he had a physical with the NFL. Although his results stated that he had extremely high cholesterol and needed to do something about that quickly, everything else registered as being acceptable. Because he was 41, they only performed an electrocardiogram (EKG), which showed no indication of a heart issue. The EKG measures the electrical activity of the heartbeat. They did not feel it was necessary to do an echocardiogram, also called an echo, which measures the action of the heart by using ultrasound waves to produce a visual display. This test would have revealed that Nate's heart was 90 percent blocked, and his left ventricle was so enlarged that it could barely pump anymore.

About six weeks after my visit to the morgue, the first autopsy results came back from the LA coroner. The doctor shared that Nate's main cause of death was a massive heart attack caused by cardiomyopathy of the left ventricle. Cardiomyopathy is a disease of the heart muscle that makes it harder to pump blood to the body. Over time and with stress (or heavy exercise and exertion), the heart becomes very big and strong. That may be good for a bicep or a glute, but it's not good for a heart. Once a heart gets too large and the muscle is too tough, it simply can't pump. When the hard muscle loses its flexibility, that can lead to heart failure. In Nate's case, it was obvious—his left ventricle was so stretched out and enlarged that it simply could no longer pump effectively.

In addition to the structure of his heart, they also found extreme plaque buildup and blockage in his arteries. During his career, he spent a combined 11 years playing on the defensive line, first at UNC and then in the NFL. The entire time he played, he tried to keep his weight around 300 pounds. He force-fed himself and was constantly trying to bulk up. If he wanted to make a team and play in a game, he needed to be big.

Anyone that knew Nate understood that he lived in extremes. Moderation was a dirty word to Nate. He was famous for fasting in February, which he liked to call his spring cleanse. But in September, once the football season started, and especially if the Yankees made it into the postseason, he would fall off the wagon and straight into a plate of nachos.

I struggled to reconcile how he could seem so healthy on the outside while being so damaged on the inside. Did football teach him to block out the pain? Had he been trained to just ignore any messages from his body that he didn't like?

The last time I saw him was when he took me to the airport before I left for Jamaica. When we got to the terminal, he parked the car and grabbed my hand. He said, "I love you so much. Go have fun and learn as much as you can. The kids and I will be fine. All is well. See you on Sunday." I wonder if he wasn't feeling well and was hiding it from me. Maybe he knew something was wrong with his heart. Maybe he was scared. All I know for sure is that four days later he was gone.

The kids remember everything from that morning. They had all woken up early, and Nate had made them breakfast. He told them that they were going to do something fun together, just the three of them.

They all got dressed and headed to Sky Zone trampoline park, 20 minutes away on the 405 freeway.

"We walked in and went to the screens to sign the waivers, but Dad couldn't get the screens to work," Jack explained. He said that Nate had gotten frustrated and yelled at the computers. Jack took over the signing-in process and noticed that "Dad seemed a little off." Eventually they completed the waivers, got their orange sticky socks to keep from slipping and began to jump on the trampolines.

For the next 10 minutes or so, he and the kids were happily jumping on a trampoline together. They were laughing, shooting baskets, and doing tricks. Then Addison yelled to him, "Daddy, Daddy, look at me!" but he didn't seem to hear. She started to walk over to him and noticed he didn't look good. The last thing that Nate said to Addison was, "I need to sit down." He then grabbed his heart and fell to the ground. He landed on the trampoline and never moved again. Addison told me later, "At first I thought Dad was joking around. I was embarrassed and told him to get up. I kneeled down next to him and said, 'Dad! Get up. Get up!' but he didn't move."

Addison called for her brother, who ran over and kneeled down next to Nate. As Jack looked closer, he could see foam coming from his mouth and that Nate was beginning to turn purple. He looked pleadingly into his father's eyes one last time and said, "Dad, please, please wake up." He told me it was the first and only time he had ever looked in his father's eyes and his Dad didn't look back.

After that, everything moved quickly. A man noticed that something was wrong and that the kids needed help. He ran to Nate and called for two other men. As they tried to roll Nate over, another mom who was there quickly ushered the kids away into a room that was saved for birthday parties. At first the men thought he had torn an ACL or suffered a seizure, but as they moved him onto his back, they realized he had no pulse. They began CPR. The staff quickly cleared everyone out of that area and called 911.

The paramedics arrived five minutes later and took over doing CPR while setting up the defibrillator. They shocked him a few times; supposedly, his heart came back faintly each time. Once he was in the ambulance, the paramedics continued to work on Nate. They said he looked like a healthy man, so his collapse didn't make sense. Over and over, his heart would try to start again and then stop. Upon arrival at UCLA Torrance, the ER team worked feverishly on him for another 20 minutes.

They said the whole team was giving him everything they had.

Defeated and tired, the lead physician finally told the team to stop. Nate was declared dead on 11/11 at 11 am. The ER doctor told me that when he found out Nate was 42, he was surprised. "He looked much older than that to me," he said. "More tired and worn out."

Through my research, I learned that in 1990, the NFL Players Association (NFLPA) requested that researchers from the National Institute for Occupational Safety and Health (NIOSH) look at the rate and causes of death among NFL players[1].

The findings were sobering.

The study included 3,439 men who played in the NFL for at least five years between 1959 and 1988. An article written by the CDC about this study states, "Defensive linemen had a 42 percent higher risk of death from heart disease compared to men in the general population. A total of 41 defensive linemen died of heart disease, when we anticipated 29 based on estimates from the general population."

The doctor from the LA coroner who performed Nate's autopsy explained to me, "Today in the NFL, the lineman need to be bigger, stronger, and more aggressive than ever before. That means their hearts will have to work even harder and pump even faster than ever before. And with that type of stress and overuse, a heart that is meant to live for 80 years may give out decades before that."

PART TWO
THE HEALING

ELEVEN
DARK NIGHTS

"There is no pain so great as the memory of joy in present grief."

-Aeschylus

After hearing the autopsy results, taking care of many logistical items and finding myself with fewer distractions, I entered a new phase of the grieving process. I felt heartbroken that Nate had been so sick and possibly feeling terrible for a long time. I couldn't reconcile the man I loved with the autopsy report I was given. One was a vibrant, healthy man, and the other was someone who may have needed a heart transplant to live. Nothing made sense, and I missed him more each day.

One night, scrunched up on my bed, trying to find a comfortable position, I felt like I needed a weighted blanket or someone to swaddle me to stop the pain. I tucked my legs under my butt and laid back, finding myself in some weird, uncomfortable semi-yoga pose. I reached my arms behind me, crossed them at the elbows and lodged them under my head. I looked like a pretzel, but the deep painful stretch gave me a minute of relief. It was 4 am, and I felt like I was going insane. My entire body hurt. In the darkness of that moment, I thought I wasn't going to make it. I didn't know if I had what I needed to survive this level of pain. For the first time in my life, I truly understood utter desperation. I forced myself out of bed and walked to the kitchen to make some tea. When I checked on the kids, I saw they had fallen asleep.

That evening had been brutal. Both of the kids were inconsolable and had screamed or cried before falling asleep. When I thought about the three of us and what our future looked like, I couldn't see any good outcome. Without Nate, there was no guiding force, no safety, no moral compass—I simply couldn't go on like this forever.

I had never uttered the words "I want to die" in a non-joking manner. For years, I had said things like, "If you make me go to lunch with those girls, I'll die" or "I would rather die than volunteer at the ice cream social." But not until this moment did I know what it really meant to want to check out for good.

In my head, I rationalized that these suicidal thoughts were appropriate based on the situation. The exhaustion from grief coupled with the devastation that was hanging over me made me feel hopeless. The nights were so long and lonely. I caught myself thinking, "I just need to get to Nate—once I find him, he will know what to do next."

For a few hours that night, I sat up in bed and thought about how best to end this thing. We simply needed some relief. I wanted it to be painless—no drama or grand statement. I just wanted to die and take the kids with me. Then at least we would all four be together again.

As I thought about it for a while, it seemed like all the options for killing us were too complicated, and I couldn't come up with a solid plan. My first idea was to calmly pull into our garage, turn on the exhaust and listen to Mozart as we breathed in carbon monoxide. But since we had recently converted our garage into a guesthouse for friends and family, that wouldn't work. There was no place to park, and the Suburban would never fit through the new French doors.

The next thought I had was overmedicating my kids. But since they were both afraid of swallowing pills, we would have to use a liquid. How many children's bubblegum-flavored Motrin would it take? I quickly realized they would quit after the first cup. So much for overdosing. And because I am extremely anti-guns, shooting them and then myself was out of the question. It definitely wasn't peaceful, and I didn't want to send the wrong political message. The only other choice I could come up with was driving off a cliff *Thelma & Louise* style, and that seemed too aggressive.

I never knew that choosing how to die could be so much work.

Finally, I settled on the idea that I could *possibly* hold them underwater in the tub. I was desperate. Night after night, I watched them writhe in emotional and physical pain, and there was nothing I could do to help them.

When the sun went down, the pain came up.

My logical brain knew I just needed this as an option. And I mostly just needed to tell this truth to someone, to speak it out loud and take the power of the lonely thoughts away. Wise decision or not, I decided to tell one of my kids because maybe we were all feeling the same way.

I couldn't share my idea with Addison—she was still so young and struggling to even understand this was real. Her pain and fear translated into her being attached to me at every moment of the day. She was scared of losing me. She was learning how to comprehend death, and she did *not* want to talk about any of it. They were almost three years apart, and their experiences were very different.

I knew Jack fully understood what happened, and I knew he was trying to be strong for Addison and me. I wanted him to know that I was also hurting but also trying to lighten the pain with some humor.

"Sweetie, I'm thinking of killing us all because this pain is too big. I feel like we may collapse under it—it might be best to just end it all. What do you think?"

He looked at me with his wise 12-year-old face and

gave me a slight smirk. "What happened to us being strong?" he asked. "And what about how lucky we are to have been loved by him? Did you forget all of those positive thoughts that you tell us a hundred times a day?"

I sat down on his bed and gave him a huge hug. "Oh, sweetie, I'm sorry to tell you this, but I lied. I was wrong. We are screwed."

We both laughed, and then he said, "Mom, sometimes I want to die, too. But I'm not sure it's the best idea. What is your brilliant plan?"

I said, "The best I could come up with was to drown you both when you're taking a bath. How does that sound?"

"Well," he said, "it doesn't sound great for a couple of reasons. First, I don't take baths anymore. Second, you only let us fill it up two inches because of the drought. It would be tough to drown someone in such shallow water. But I love you, Mom."

Before he walked out, he gave me a kiss and said, "And don't forget, I'm three inches taller and 20 pounds heavier than you. I will never let you hold me down."

We hugged for longer than normal, then headed back to our rooms.

A few weeks later, Jack and I were talking before he went to bed.

"Mom, on some days, I think if I had a gun, I would end it," he told me.

Those words terrified me. I wasn't exactly sure what to say, but I was glad we had spoken about suicide and this feeling of hopelessness before. I immediately called his therapist and asked what to do. She was calm and told me it was normal. "He's so scared and sad," she said. "Let him talk about it but keep him away from guns."

So I listened to him talk, and I made sure he didn't get near a gun. I tried to control my fear and reminded myself that he, like all of us, deeply wanted relief and to have Nate back. I never judged him for it or tried to talk him out of it. Instead, we just sat in his pain and let it be. I kept asking him to hold on for another day or another week and see if there was any more space.

As I lay in my bed that night, I thought about the gifts of my kids, my conversations with my son and our shared desperation. In some new way, after the day's events, I felt relief from the pain. We had found a way to share our darkest thoughts with humor and honesty—the words we didn't want to share or say out loud—and it became one of the very best ways to heal. During that first year, I knew if we could find the courage to share our darkest thoughts, we might just be okay. Maybe one day, we might even be exceptional.

TWELVE
THE THERAPY

"We cannot do everything at once, but we can do something at once."
- Calvin Coolidge

When I was 15, my parents got separated. My mom wanted me to go talk to someone and "process" this new living situation. As luck would have it, my appointments were on Friday afternoons—not the ideal activity to start the weekend for a teenager, plus my therapist was a very odd character. I remember hating it, but I also remember that she loved cats, wore beaded necklaces and that she helped me.

Therapy was a gift my mom loved to give me. After Nate and I got engaged, we went to visit her in Florida. "I have something special I want to give you as you start your life together," she told us one day. I was hoping it was a vacuum cleaner because ours had just died. While most of my friends had received presents like Cuisinart Blenders or framed engagement photos, my mom announced, "Your gift is a three-day intensive therapy retreat based on Imago Therapy and the book *Getting the Love You Want* by Harville Hendrix." I didn't see that coming, and by the look on Nate's face, neither did he. He seemed confused, maybe because he was hoping for a grill, or maybe because he realized what type of family he was marrying into. She gave us the printed itinerary for the event, and we both squeaked out, "Thank you?"

Even though a Days Inn motel in Longwood, Florida, wasn't our dream getaway, that weekend in 2002 changed our relationship for the better. It gave us a lot of tools that we used during our marriage as well as a deeper understanding of what exactly each of us "brought to the party" in our relationship. The workshop was interesting, and so were the participants. We were by far the youngest couple there, as well as the only couple who wasn't attending as a last-ditch effort to save their marriage from divorce. People kept asking, "Why are you two here again?" and Nate would answer with a confused look on his face, "I have no idea; it was an engagement gift."

Always a good sport and a man willing to do the internal work, Nate dug in with me. We analyzed our childhood, our parents and how those relationships informed how we experienced ours. We looked at our communication styles and learned more effective ways to talk. It was strange, enlightening and very impactful. Therapy and counseling weren't our favorite pastimes, but we relied on those skills often.

After Nate died, I knew we needed help and needed it fast. Although I was focused on getting back to joy and laughter, that didn't mean I wasn't seriously depressed, suicidal and scared out of my mind. I understood that books, prayers and positive affirmations wouldn't be enough. So I threw myself and the kids into therapy—a lot of it. The ability to do this was something I didn't take for granted. It takes a lot of resources and time to do the type of therapy we did, and I am clear that most people don't have access to this in the same way. During that first year, because of the benefits Nate had accrued as a player, much of our talk therapy was paid for by the NFL. I am grateful that the organization supported us in this area, and I think every employer should value this resource the same way. Everyone deserves to be supported through trauma and hardship. The therapy we received changed our lives and helped us move forward.

I was open to anything and tried everything: craniosacral therapy, psychosomatic therapy, sound healing, plant medicine and deep tissue massage at a Korean spa. I floated in tanks. I tapped on my face to release emotional stress and anxiety, which is called EFT or Emotional Freedom Technique. I did acupuncture. I attended grief groups. I was having an around-the-world journey of ways to heal.

I started with a bereavement therapist because I thought I needed an expert in the area of loss, and going to a specialist sounded like the right idea. I was hoping that she would have her own personal experience of navigating loss and living through grief that she could share with me. I wanted to know what she had done and what insights she could share that would help me to survive.

The therapist's name was Judith. I had never seen a bereavement therapist before, but if you had asked me to cast one for a movie, I would have chosen her right away. She had long, curly brown hair, big sad eyes, a soft voice and a makeup-free face. She was earthy and talked slowly and looked like someone who would rescue cats in six-packs. Her office smelled lightly of incense, and there were dream catchers hanging from various plants. From the start, I knew there was a disconnect between us. I wasn't sure if it was just an energy thing or if we were truly orbiting on different planets.

She began by asking me to "share my story." I hadn't been talking for long, maybe two minutes, and she started to cry. And I mean crying hard. I was so confused, and I was getting annoyed. She kept blowing her nose and saying, "Oh my God, this is so sad." I already knew it was sad; I needed her to help me see the other side. I was starting to think that might not happen. At one point, in the middle of talking about finding out he was gone, I had to stop and ask her if *she* was okay. At that moment, I should have left. But I had so little energy, was so tired and the damn couch was so comfortable that I kept going.

During a break in our dialogue, I asked, "Have you ever lost someone who is close to you?"

Based on her emotional reaction, I was certain she would say yes and that something I said had triggered her own pain.

"No," she said, "I have never lost anyone. But my beloved dog died in 2015."

I muttered under my breath, "You have got to be fucking kidding me."

We talked for a little longer, and then our hour was up. After I finished, I gave *her* a tissue. She blew her nose, found her composure and then handed me a worksheet titled "Common Emotions During Grief." She wanted me to circle the ones I had felt and told me, "At some point, you will feel all of these, and it's going to get *bad*." I wanted her to have her therapy license revoked.

I looked at the worksheet, read all the "feeling" words and simply circled the entire paper. I handed it to her and said, "Now what?"

She nodded. "Okay interesting, seems like you have a lot of feelings but don't forget you are still numb. This is just the beginning. In two or three months, it's going to get worse. The second year is *bad*!" I looked at her and wished I could circle the word "disbelief" 20 times.

That was the end of that client/therapist relationship, but next, I found someone who could help. Samantha was a free spirit who did bodywork and talk therapy. She knew what she was doing, and so did her three small dogs. These animals, who were saved from being slaughtered in China, always started the session sitting at my feet. When I began to struggle or cry, one or two or all of them came to sit in my lap. Samantha said they followed their own hearts and only engaged when they were called to do so. I started to feel anxiety if I had gone too long without one of them feeling the call to my soul, but most days ended with at least one head in my lap. It was odd, and it was so very LA, and for reasons I still don't understand, it helped me a lot.

During our second session, Samantha said, "Kelsey, it's interesting that you seem to be very focused on Nate and how he's doing. You are concerned with him more than anyone else right now."

I agreed with her.

Samantha continued, "Do you ever think that maybe because he is dead, he doesn't feel human emotions anymore?"

I had never considered that. In my mind, I pictured all of our family and friends in the courtyard of some hotel. We were drinking and laughing, but Nate couldn't get to us. He was stuck on the top floor desperately trying to get to our party, and I felt terrible for him.

But her question made me think about Nate in a different way.

It was a small shift, but it was a huge awakening for me. I didn't have to know anything. I just had to trust that he was *okay*. If I could do that, then maybe I could start focusing on the kids and myself a little bit more.

Later that day, I had a talk with Nate. "Hey love,

turns out I have no idea where the hell you are or what you are doing," I said. "I wish I had more answers, but I don't. So I'm going to trust that you are okay—hopefully even exceptional. I'm going to let go of worrying about you. I pray you are having the time of your life and only feeling love."

This was the first time I had considered that "I don't know" might be a perfectly acceptable place to be. I had spent my life trying to know everything, to have all the answers, or at least pretend to have them. When I made this mental switch, I gave up the idea that I had to know how to do this or where I was going. I let go of trying to figure everything out. This experience, how I felt, what I did or didn't do, where Nate was, all of it didn't need to fit in little boxes.

Many people ask me what I know or believe about death. What worked for me was to create a story around death and the people who died that gave me peace. I think that is one reason religion speaks so deeply to people. It provides answers to questions that really are unknowable. In doing so, it creates a road map or a foundation that gives stability to many parts of life that don't make sense. I realized I didn't have any answers, but I was excited about all the different possibilities.

During one of my last sessions, Samantha suggested one more thing. "Kelsey, why don't you write Nate a letter. Tell him everything you would have wanted to say." Writing a letter seemed brilliant because there was so much I never got to share. "And also," she continued, "write a letter to yourself from Nate, making sure he says to you everything you know he would want you to hear."

Here's what I wrote:

Dear Nate,

As I am sure you know, dying was a terrible idea. Some days I feel so much physical pain from not being able to hug you or speak to you that I can't move. I'm so grateful that our last conversation and texts were so kind. You were my best friend, the person I knew better than anyone else, and now I am trying to comprehend that I will never see you again.

Today I was driving around LA in circles because I couldn't think. I have been so strong and so positive, but now I'm over it, and it turns out I'm super angry with you.

Our entire marriage, you called me the "fun police." You told me I needed to relax, to have fun and live in the moment. How the hell was I supposed to live in the moment when I could feel something bad was happening? Who dies in front of their kids at a trampoline park? I thought you were healthy and we were going to live the rest of our lives together.

Now it's the holidays, and I'm alone with our kids and both our moms, and I have no idea how the hell I got here. I used to ask you all the time, "You will never leave us, right? We will always be okay?" And you wouldn't miss a beat in replying, "Of course! You are the greatest part of my life. I will always take care of you."

Now you are on the way to the Divine, which is what you always said you wanted. "I can't wait to get to Heaven and just relax!" you would joke. But now you're there, and I have another 50 years to navigate this life without you. It's hard to breathe some days.

But the hardest part is this: I have loved you since the day I met you. I miss you so much and have no idea how to do this without you. We need you here. Especially the kids. They love you so much. They want to see their dad. Without you in our lives, nothing seems right.

But I wouldn't change a thing, and I will figure this all out. The pleasure was worth the pain.

You were the best man I have ever known. Rest easy, sweet man.

Here's the letter from Nate to me:

Dear Kelsey,

First, you need to know I have always thought you were the strongest woman I have ever met. I waited my whole life to see you become the person you are today. You have gifts that you are just now recognizing and a strength that is going to blow your mind.

I'm deeply sorry I couldn't stay in the physical realm to see it with you, but I will always be cheering you on from the most exquisite place I have ever been. You don't need to worry about me anymore. I am where I've always wanted to be in the Divine. I have no emotional or physical pain. I am at peace. It's amazing here, and I look forward to seeing you and the kids in what will seem like a blink.

I loved you from the first day I met you. There was no one else I wanted to do life with than you. You are the funniest, smartest, and most beautiful woman I have ever seen. I loved every minute of our life together.

Please don't be afraid! It's your turn. You have everything you need to make the rest of your life be beyond your wildest imagination. The kids are going to be great! That is why I spent so much time talking to them, even though it bugged you. I gave them everything they needed from me, and I promise I wouldn't have left if that weren't true. They get it, and they are extraordinary humans!

Now that you don't have to watch over and worry about me, I want you to go have fun. Go! Live life fully the way I did. It's the best! Meet people, go places and have great sex. You'll know the right person when they arrive. If you so choose, you will have a fulfilling and exceptional life with them. Until then, just keep doing your thing.

I know it's hard to believe, but the four of us are all exactly where we are meant to be. I know you can feel that deep in your soul; on some level, both you and the kids know this is true. The day we met in college, you and I both knew we had signed up for a different and challenging journey, but also one that would be exceptional. We both were always looking for more than a regular, comfortable life.

Kelsey, I will always be here for you. I know how safe and protected I made you feel. Please know that I'm not gone, and you are not alone. Remember when you told me you loved me because you knew that if a tsunami hit, I would become a whale and carry you all on my back? You were right, so just keep holding on. I got you still. I love you forever, in this realm and the next.

Sometimes I have to say to myself what I dream other people would say. Some days, that has to be enough.

THIRTEEN

PRESENT MOMENTS

"Be still and listen to the stillness within."

- Darlene Larson Jenks

It was 9:20 am on a September day, and I was utterly exhausted. So far, all I had done that day was wake up, make breakfast for the kids and drive them to school. Yet at that moment, all of it felt like a Herculean task. I looked at the dirty dishes and said out loud, "Nate, you get them." And then I crawled back in bed.

I woke up an hour later, and my mind told me I had to do something productive. Maybe brush my hair, fold laundry, send an email, anything that would require me to move. But I didn't listen. Instead I walked to the couch, lay down and slept again. I must have slept for a while because when I opened my eyes, I felt rested. When I looked at the clock, I realized soon the kids would need to be picked up, so I jumped in the shower and washed my hair. But right before I turned off the water, I found myself sliding down onto the floor. I needed the hot water to pour over me for just a little longer.

When the adrenaline of tragedy wore off, about six months after he had died, I found myself catatonic. It didn't keep me from living, but it was like living underwater. I would take one exhausted step after the next. As time went by, I realized that sleep was my medicine, and I took a lot of it. When I slept, there was no panic in my mind or ache in my body. And if I was lucky, I often dreamed about Nate. It was my happy place, but I knew I couldn't sleep forever; there was a life to be lived and children to raise.

Raising two kids alone gave me a lot of purpose but very little peace. If I was crying in the bathroom, someone would knock and yell, "Mom, can you help me with math?" When I was lying on the floor, pretending to do yoga, I would hear, "Mom, have you seen my cleats?" And the moment I sat down at the end of the night to mindlessly watch something on TV, a kid would ask, "Mom, will you help me make some food?" The requests never stopped but neither did my thoughts or my sadness.

Addison was now in fifth grade, and she was working hard to stay focused and trying to enjoy her last year in elementary. One morning later that week, she said,

"Mom, don't forget you have your parent-teacher conference today with Mr. Heck," as she headed out the door. I looked at her, smiled and said, "Looking forward to it, have a great day."

That afternoon, I drove to the school and parked in an illegal drop off spot because it was closer to the building. Mr. Heck is an exceptional teacher, one of the best I have ever known, and he was waiting for me outside the classroom. "Come in Mrs. Chittick," he said as we sat down and he began his presentation about Addison's progress. As I was sitting at the tiny table in a classroom that smelled like crayon and glue, I had a visceral desire to slide off the blue plastic chair and underneath the table. I pictured myself pleading with him, "I'm so sorry, but I'm gonna need to lie down while you talk. My eyes are going to be closed, but I promise you I'm sort of listening. Please continue telling me how she is doing with fractions."

I had to find a new way to recharge—a place where my mind and body could rest.

GRIEF FELT VERY physical for me. There were days my body felt exhausted, as if I had done an hour of boot camp. The energy grieving required was overwhelming. And it wasn't just my body; my brain was on overdrive, and its ability to loop on thoughts and unrealized fears was extraordinary.

Which may explain why I became militant about meditation.

A few weeks after Nate died, I started reading a lot of books. I wanted to know everything about death, grief and how people survive losing someone they love. I read Christian authors, spiritual authors and many books about Buddhism. I found myself gravitating toward books that focused on meditation and Buddhist practices. One day, I picked up a book that had been on my nightstand forever. As I opened *When Things Fall Apart* by Pema Chodron, I thought, "Now that's a great title! Exactly how I feel!" It was the same with *Radical Acceptance by* Tara Brach. I dug in.

Both of these books focused on meditation and the process of getting through hard times. Along with giving me some practical ways to recharge and relax, they taught me a lot about supporting my kids on their journey through this pain. Each author explored the practice of releasing the desire to try to make a singular moment better. Instead, they suggested that through breathwork and meditation, we can learn to switch our focus from fixing the problem to simply being present with "what is." And when we do that, when we can stay in the present moment, with ourselves or others—when we hold that pain and honor it—healing begins.

I couldn't sleep at stoplights or during meetings but, I realized, I could find ways to stop my mind and rest my body. Meditation was the key, and it allowed me to reset my nervous system anytime, anywhere.

It gave me space from the pain, a blank place to rest in. Most days after I meditated, I was fully convinced we were going to be okay. Some days it was easier than others, but typically when I slowed down and tapped into God or the Divine, the message I received was clear.

"All is well. I am right where I need to be."

Through meditation, I realized that it wasn't his actual death that was causing me pain; it was the way I was thinking about his death. If I stopped labeling his death as "bad," I could begin to find joy in a very tough and painful situation.

The longer I sat still and the more I focused on my breath, the easier it was to find a new perspective. And in those moments, time would stand still, and an awareness would wash over me that this wouldn't last forever. I understood that this time in my life, this painful experience, was only a nanosecond compared to the entire journey of my soul.

I can handle anything for a nanosecond.

Meditation was my lifeboat, and my breath was my oars. (Cheesiest sentence ever, but that shit is true). I started meditating every day. At first, it was something I *needed* to do. Then it became something I *wanted* to do. Then it became something I had to do in order to live the life I wanted to live.

I started craving meditation the same way I craved cheese quesadillas, French fries and sleep. I looked forward to getting up and sitting cross-legged on my bed or on the couch before the kids woke up, when the house was still quiet. I looked forward to waiting in the car to pick them up from school and closing my eyes for a minute and breathing it all in. I loved sitting outside in the morning sun, eyes closed, palms open and quieting my mind. That is the place I felt safe and where my fear faded away. When I blocked out the world and focused on getting air in and out of my lungs, I could find peace.

But my meditation and Buddhist practices didn't just help me; they also helped me support my children. Watching my kids in pain was gut-wrenching, and for a while, I struggled with how to help them. But then I came upon this mantra, and it changed everything.

"I see you."

"I hear you."

"I'm so sorry you are suffering."

"I'm here for you. Always."

Typically, when my kids would start to cry, panic or scream, I would try to fix it all. "He was the best dad; you are so lucky he was yours, and look how good our life still is," I would say as they screamed louder. No matter what I said, nothing helped.

One day I felt unusually overwhelmed. I was barely hanging on, and I didn't have any energy left for the kids. I was scared. I prayed the night would be an easy one, but as we started to get ready for bed, I could feel their sadness, and I knew they needed me to be present with their pain. I begged to God, "Please not tonight, God not tonight. I'm too tired to help them, and I am out of wisdom or hope." As if in answer to my prayers, Jack came in, gave me a hug and said he was headed off to bed. One down.

Addison wasn't doing as well. She had that restless look in her eye and kept asking me to lie with her. I knew she wanted to talk, but I was so exhausted. When I climbed in bed and lay down next to her, she started to cry, "Mama, I miss my daddy. I want my daddy to put me to bed." I knew what was coming; we had done this so many times. I started to do what I had always done, but then I remembered one of the chapters I had just read. Now I had a plan. I took a minute to breathe and sink into my body. I focused on my breath and getting out of my head. Next, I put a hand on her arm and stayed quiet. As she screamed, I just let her work through it, no matter how hard or painful it was to watch. I didn't try to stop it or make it end—I just sat there.

With my hand over her tiny heart, she eventually quieted down. And then she closed her eyes, and I whispered to her:

"I see you, sweetie. Addison, I hear you. I'm so sorry you are suffering. I'm here for you. Always."

I kept repeating those words, and her breathing slowed down. I could feel her body relax. It was like watching her emerge from a huge storm, battered and tired but still alive. Finally she grabbed my hand and said, "Thanks, Mom. I feel better. I want to go to bed."

That night I learned that showing up for my kids

didn't mean I had to fix anything or say anything brilliant. It meant I had to be present with them as they experienced whatever they were going through. From then on, no matter what emotional state I was in, I knew I could help them.

FOURTEEN
REFRAME OR GO INSANE

"Acceptance is knowing that grief is a raging river. And you have to get into it, because when you do, it carries you to the next place. It eventually takes you to open land, somewhere where in the end, it will turn out okay."

– Simone George

"Why me? This isn't fair!" I screamed at the top of my lungs while driving down the Pacific Coast Highway to Target. "How can this be my life?!"

I was furious that I was a widow, and I wanted my old life back. As I pulled into the parking lot, I saw the big Target Bullseye and a line of red shopping carts. Normally, Target was my happy place, but not that day.

Even the call of the fluorescent lights and long aisles of retail therapy couldn't help. I had fallen into one of my "poor me" moments.

I put the car in park and looked at myself in the mirror. It wasn't a pretty sight. No makeup, just yesterday's smudged mascara. My hair was greasy, my skin was dry and my eyes looked like I had been in a boxing match.

"I hate my life," I said to the mirror. And then I took a breath. I had been here before, and I was getting better at navigating these expected moments of discomfort. "I don't hate my life," I corrected myself, "but I really miss Nate."

As I said those new words out loud, my brain clicked in with support. "Kelsey, this is your life. Choose a better story to tell," I heard from some deep part of my soul. I was never sure if that voice was mine, or maybe Nate's or God's, but when it didn't annoy the shit out of me, it helped me feel better.

Earlier that morning, when I was walking Addison into school, I did what I always did. I tried to ignore every single human that walked by me. I would pretend I was on the phone, talking to my kid or just looking in the other direction. But somehow that morning, an overeager mom snuck into my personal space.

"Kelsey, it's so good to see you," she said with the sad face I had come to know well. "We think about you and the kids all the time. How *are* you doing?"

Addison tried to rush me along. She hated these

conversations even more than I did. But I stopped to be polite and because I was always grateful that people cared enough to ask.

There was an innate problem with that question. I had no idea how I was doing; my feelings changed every second. Early on, I learned to answer automatically. I said the same thing every time, with the same tone and the same fake smile.

"Well, we are doing it. Thanks for asking," I said to the woman, and I could tell she felt better. I asked her about her kids, and then the bell rang. Thankfully the conversation was over. As we headed to her classroom, Addison grabbed my arm and said with an annoyed tone, "Mom, why do you answer like that? You say the same stupid thing every time!"

She was right. I was on autopilot a lot of the time, especially with people I didn't know that well. I felt bad for them (and for myself) because the topic of dead dads is uncomfortable. They aren't conversations you want to have for too long. But Addison's question had made me think. Why *did* I keep saying the same thing, especially when it wasn't even true? The kids were listening to my answers, and the truth was, we were doing damn well considering what we had been through. Of course it was hard and sad and lonely, but we were doing a lot more than just "doing it." We were fighting for joy every day.

I told myself from now on, that was the story, I was going to share. Not the one I thought people wanted to hear. The words I chose mattered, not just for me but for my kids. I was the one who got to create the meaning this had in our lives. I was the author of this story and I had an important job to do. I needed to make this story a good one. Our lives depended on it.

Creating a story was something I had been training for my whole life. As a kid, I loved telling stories. I did and said whatever it took to make people laugh and feel good. Later, as a stand-up comic, I looked for the funny in every situation, especially the hard ones. And as a speaker, I valued the *feeling* a story conveyed way more than the facts.

I wanted to speak about Nate's death and tell the story in a specific way, one that always moved us forward. Being truthful, but also focusing on the parts that allowed us to take our power back. Reframing the story allowed us to reflect on this event with a hopeful perspective, one that allowed us to feel supported and more in control. It forced us to look at what was good in our lives and do our best to focus on the parts where our gratitude for having Nate overrode the pain.

Of course, there were *tons* of days when the grief got in the way. Days when it was so dark and scary that the only story I wanted to share is "*We are so screwed*!" But if we commit to believing something and say it and share it often, it becomes the default story that we believe most of the time. It took work but, for us, it was worth it.

This is the story I started telling people who asked how we were doing.

"Well, I got to spend 21 years with the greatest man

in the world and now have his amazing children. He died before we wanted or expected, and boy do we miss him so much. But we are so grateful for having him, and we are committed to enjoying our lives. We know that is the best way to honor him."

Our ability to reframe these events wasn't just helping me; it was helping the kids. Soon after his dad died, Jack agreed to go to therapy once a week. He was committed to the work and told me many times, "Mom, counseling really helps me." During those sessions, he dug in, he cried, he screamed, and he talked about everything that was on his mind. I asked why he liked it so much, and he said, "She helps me work through how I feel about Dad. And truthfully, she's the only woman that really listens to me." We both laughed so hard. As time went on, I could almost see the pain, depression and fear work themselves out of him. He, too, was making a choice on how he wanted to understand and experience his dad's death.

One day I picked him up from soccer practice. He got in the car, sweaty and tired as usual, but he seemed different. Typically, at pickup, he would seem sullen or sad, but today he seemed lighter. "How was your practice?" I asked. And he replied, "You know what? It went great." I asked him what was different. "Well, I decided to be happy again," he said. "I started to joke with my friends and be a leader. For so long, I have either been so sad or thought people needed me to be sad that I lost myself.

But today, I went back to being my old self and it felt great!" And then he paused for a minute. "And I also realized that playing sports is more fun now. I loved it when Dad watched me play, but whenever I made a mistake, he and I would look at each other, and I knew I had let him down. Now I get to play sports without worrying about what he thinks of how I play. In some ways, that's a great gift I never expected."

I did my best to respond calmly, the way you do with teenagers so that you don't spook them or make them stop sharing. I didn't want him to know how deeply moved I was by his words. So as quietly as I could, I simply looked at him and said, "You're pretty special. What an awesome and unexpected gift! Thank you for sharing."

All of us were working through this experience and trying to understand what it meant to us and our future. Everyone's path was different, and everyone got to decide how they wanted it to define them. Because Addison was nine when Nate died, she was just starting to comprehend the finality of death and what it all meant. Developmentally she was still in the "magical thinking" stage. Magical thinking is a child's belief that what he or she wishes or expects can affect what really happens. It would be a few years before we would really see how she would decide to process grief and define his death.

Reframing the story didn't mean we avoided the pain, missed the lessons, or got to bypass the hard parts. The exact opposite was true. Reframing meant we flowed with what was and didn't offer any resistance. We let it all in. We went to the darkest and deepest depths of our souls and faced our grief. And then, once it had moved through us, we found the strength and courage to stand up again.

FIFTEEN
TALK TO ME

"Grief never ends...but it changes. It's a passage, not a place to stay. Grief is not a sign of weakness, nor a lack of faith. It is the price of love."
- Unknown

At 6:15 on Tuesday morning, I heard my alarm go off. I hit snooze and laid there for a few more minutes. I never felt more peaceful than I did in the first few minutes of each morning; the dreams of the night were still close by, and my nervous system was rested and calm.

The house was quiet, everyone was still asleep and I could take deep breaths with no anxiety present. "Thank you, God!" I thought to myself. My kids were home and safe, but no one was talking to me or fighting about anything. I have always been a morning person, but over the last few years, I've treasured this time more than ever.

That morning, I pulled the covers off and walked into the bathroom, wearing no bra and my favorite old ratty PJs. I slid my glasses off my swollen face and took out my dirty bun. I brushed my teeth, put in my contacts and stared directly into the bathroom mirror. It was a frightening sight. Standing there half-awake, make-up free, under the harsh glow of overhead lights took courage. All I saw was a tired, middle-aged widow who wanted to go back to bed.

But I didn't let that face get me down. I knew what I needed to do that could help her immediately.

1. Call a dermatologist and schedule a full LA Botox experience. No skimping; I needed the full Monty.
2. Make an appointment to have my hairdresser pour bleach all over my head and then put me under a heat fan. Highlights always make me feel better.
3. Talk to myself. That needed to start now.

I stared into the toothpaste-smeared bathroom mirror, and I began my ritual:

"I am beautiful. I am smart. I am funny. I am healthy. I have more money than I've ever dreamed. I have a joyful life. My kids are safe and thriving. I serve others each day. I have a beautiful home that I love. I love to travel and enjoy meeting the most amazing people."

I said those sentences five times each until the words started to blend together. Some of those words were true, and some I planned on becoming true in the future.

Did I feel weird looking into the mirror, talking to myself? Yes.

Did I think I might have lost my mind or belonged at a Tony Robbins retreat? Yes.

Did I feel fake or cheesy or weird as I repeated these phrases aloud? Yes.

So why the hell did I do it? For one reason. This shit works. It's a scientific game of tricking and training your brain. Over time, you can rewire the brain to create new pathways, ones that end with the feeling associated with the positive statement. And the more you say it, the more you believe it.

One of my favorite sayings is, "You have to believe it to see it." Not the other way around.

When I said these affirmations, even if they hadn't shown up in my life yet, there was a nanosecond when my brain thought it was true and when that happened, I began to feel and act as if that was the reality I was living in. There was a moment before my ego or conscious mind started to argue with me. Before it fired back with statements like "Nope, not true" or "Good luck, never gonna happen." My subconscious had already taken those positive words and began to integrate them into my soul. The more I said them, the more I started to believe them. And once I believed them, I could see them. Finally, what I saw became my reality, which then became my truth. BOOM! How cool is that?

Once I got the hang of it, I started forcing the kids to do the same. "*Mooommmm*, please don't make us say things again. It's *so* annoying!" they would scream from their rooms. I would threaten them with no TV or iPad or even food if they didn't read their positive affirmations out loud each day. We taped them on their bedroom mirrors and on the refrigerator door. I was fine with us being sad and miserable. I knew that was an important part of this path. But I was determined not to let us get stuck there for too long.

That song from months ago, "Three Little Birds" by Bob Marley, became the theme song of our mornings. The kids pleaded with me to turn it off, but I wouldn't stop. I wasn't giving up, even when they tried to run out of the kitchen. As they were about to get out of the car each morning, I would say, "Have a great day, and don't forget...Everything is going to be alllllllrighttttttt!" They would roll their eyes and laugh, "Mom, you're insane." But I knew I was on the right path.

As expected, we toggled between good days, numb days and the awful days that come with losing someone you love. I was prepared for the sadness but what I wasn't ready for was the anger. As someone who deeply desires happy times and happy people, I had to learn how to accept the anger that came along with this experience and find a way to honor it for my kids. If I were them, and my dad had died in front of me, I would be furious also.

One Saturday morning, I knew it was going to be a hard day. Everybody was in a mood, especially the kids. No one wanted to talk, eat or find anything good about their lives. Everybody was pissed. The kids were mad, they missed their dad, and at this moment, his dying had ruined their life. Jack sulked into the kitchen and slammed the milk on the counter. Addison moped around her room while calling "Mom!" and then once I arrived, saying "Get out!" I knew one thing for sure--positive affirmations weren't going to help.

I sat in the kitchen thinking about how we were going to get through the day. As I was drinking my coffee, I picked up the paper and flipped through. My eye caught an ad I had never seen before. It was for a place in LA called the "Rage Cage." The description was interesting: "Have fun, de-stress, and break things." As someone who is always looking for signs from above, I took this ad as a flashing green light. Smashing and breaking things sounded ideal, so I grabbed my phone and looked up the site. The idea was brilliant, but the cost was ridiculous. So I came up with a different plan.

I found the kids lying miserably in their beds.

"Hey, do you all want to run to the Dollar Store with me?" I asked.

They looked up. There are few things my kids enjoy more than a trip to the Dollar Store.

"Here's the deal," I told them. "You each have $20 to

spend. But the first $15 needs to be used for ceramic plates. The remaining $5 is yours to spend as you please."

They jumped up, got dressed and we headed out the door. Forty-five minutes later, we were back in the car with 30 white ceramic dinner plates, one package of Starburst and two bags of ramen noodles.

When we got home, I parked in front of the house and gave them instructions.

"Ok, this is how it works. Everything you just bought, you have to break. You need to throw it as hard as you can and smash it into the trashcan or on the concrete." They were confused.

"Wait, what?" Jack asked, "You want us to break everything we bought?"

I grabbed one of the plates, got out of the car and headed to a concrete area next to our trash area. I lifted the plate over my head and threw it with all my strength into the garbage can. It shattered into pieces as the kids jumped out of the car, screaming with excitement.

"And one more thing," I said. "I want you to cuss. Any word, no matter how awful it is. Just throw the plates and get mad."

The kids grabbed their bags and went to work. For the next 15 minutes, we all went crazy. We threw each plate one by one and yelled our favorite cuss words.

"FUUUCK, SHITTT, DAMN IT!"

Dishes were crashing, kids were swearing, and all of us were laughing hysterically. After the last plate crumbled, we caught our breath. I smiled at them both and said, "Okay, now we are back to real life. No cussing or breaking things. I hope everyone feels a little better."

As they walked back into the house, I knew that anger had moved out—not for good but at least for that day.

There's a saying: Emotion needs motion. And I tried my best to keep those emotional waves moving in the healthiest and loudest ways.

SIXTEEN
I'M ENOUGH

"Something still exists as long as there's someone around to remember it."
- Jodi Picoult

"Who wants to play Monopoly?" Nate would bellow as he sleepily walked up the stairs. On Saturday mornings, he was famous for sleeping late. But once he woke up, he would be totally available for the kids. They would fly out from the living room where they had been watching Peppa Pig and scream, "Daddy's awake! I want to play!" As they barreled into him, he would lift them both up into his strong arms and swing them around while they screeched with joy. He was just starting his day, but I had usually been up for hours. I had already done three loads of laundry, unloaded the dishwasher, and blown off the outside leaves. The kids had been fed, and the kitchen was clean. Nate would put the kids down and come over to me. "Hello and good morning to the most beautiful woman in the world," he would say while trying to kiss my face. I would laugh and pull away. "Did you sleep a strong 10 hours my love? Must be soooo nice!" And at that point, I would hand off the parenting duties and grab a book while he took over.

The chaos of Monopoly began with the painstaking choice of what symbol to use: the shoe, the thimble or the dog. The joy on the kids' faces was evident; they adored their daddy. Nate would pour a huge cup of coffee, sit down at the table and begin organizing the paper money and the board. "Okay, who at this table can tell me the role of the Federal Reserve," he would ask. And the kids would scream, *"Federal who? Not me!"*

Nate would then begin his morning lesson, starting with finance and then moving into politics and religion. The kids would listen and ask questions, all while rolling dice, laughing and reveling in their time with their dad. And on those mornings, Nate was truly in heaven. There was no place he loved to be more than with his kids. Every now and then someone would say, "Mom, come play!" and I would respond, "No thank you, board games are my nightmare, and someone has to clean this house." And then they would chant, *"Fun. Po-lice! Fun-police!"* until I gave in.

Nate could play cards or Monopoly or Candy Land for hours. When I spend 30 minutes playing Uno, I feel like I deserve the next three years off. When he talked to the kids, he was undistracted, listening to every word without judgment or fear. When I talk to my kids, I'm also folding clothes, checking my phone, and cutting them off with unsolicited advice every three minutes. My idea of the perfect day is to have everyone in the house safe and happy while I orbit around them cleaning, organizing, or reading a book. That type of day would have been Nate's worst nightmare—he wanted to be right at the center with them, not on the edges. He loved the intensity of the time he spent with them. When he was with them, it was as if the rest of the world faded away.

When the kids were little, they would play a game called "Tackle Daddy." It wasn't a very complicated game. It went like this: Nate would go into the middle of the kitchen and sit down. Almost all of Nate's games entailed him sitting down or lying on a bed or floor. The kids would then run to their rooms which were on the other side of the house. Then they would yell to him, "*Daddy*, are you ready for me to *tackle* you??"

"I'm ready! 3-2-1 *blast off*!" he would yell back.

Once they heard that, the kids would fly into the kitchen as fast as they could and tackle him. Nate would fall over and pretend they had seriously injured him. Everyone would scream with joy. The game could go on for hours. My favorite thing was watching those three be together.

After he died, I struggled to see how I could be both a mom and dad, especially when Nate had been such a great one. We used to be a team, and it had worked out beautifully. But now we were missing someone important, and sometimes I wondered if he would be better at this than me.

The days were getting longer, and the clocks had sprung forward for daylight saving time. Losing an hour was always traumatic for Nate, and it seemed to have the same effect on his daughter.

"Sweetie, it's time to wake up," I whispered one day as I opened her blinds. She moaned back, "Mom, I'm so tired! I can't do this anymore! I have nothing to wear! I'm *not* going to *school*!" I took a breath and tried to stay calm. Her emotional outbursts had become all too common, and I prayed this wouldn't be a terrible day.

I had already started making breakfast when she walked in crying.

"*Mama*, I need you!"

Sometimes I didn't have anything to give, or I would yell back, but for some reason I stayed calm, walked over and gave her a big hug.

"Addison, let's take it one step at a time. First, let's brush your hair. Then we'll go from there." I could feel her relax.

The morning began moving forward: hair brushed, clothes on, lunch packed. I was tentatively hopeful. As we climbed into the car, she tapped my shoulder.

"Thanks, Mama—thank you for taking care of me so well."

I was stunned. I wanted to cry. I wanted to scream to

someone, "Thank you God! I. Am. Doing the thing!" But I just said, "You're welcome."

When we got to school, I geared up for the next tantrum, the one that normally happens at drop off. But she just smiled at me.

"Bye Mom, thanks for braiding my hair!" I was in shock. A morning without tears and screaming?

As I drove home, I thought about my question, about how I would do it without Nate—and I realized I had the answer. I would do it one day at a time. And then I asked myself a question that I believe every surviving spouse thinks about inside their own head.

"What would it be like if I was the one that was dead?"

I knew this much: if I died, those kids would be loved. They would be treasured. They would be raised with high morals and a great education. But, the chances of them making it to school on time, being fed or wearing clean clothes would have been lower. He would have been able to do it alone, and so would I, but he would need way more help.

That day, it clicked. I was going to believe that I was exactly what they needed. Partly because they didn't really like board games anymore and partly because it was my turn to show up. I began to celebrate my neurotic, organized, multitasking and loving self in a way I hadn't been able to before. I rested in the idea that if I did the best I could, somehow, I would be enough.

SEVENTEEN
THE JOURNEY

"If it came from a plant, eat it. If it was made in a plant, don't."

- Michael Pollan

The summer after Nate died, the kids and I needed a change of scenery. I had this deep desire to go somewhere new, somewhere far away, somewhere we could experience places we had never seen before.

Through the kindness of the people I had met in Jamaica, we received a generous invitation to go to Tallinn, Estonia, in July for an event. The event was called Mindvalley University, and it was summarized as a "transformational event that takes you to a different city each year, immersing you in a curated community of workshops, talks, and seminars."

It's like a summer school for families that rotates its campus location each year. The summer before we went, it was in Barcelona; the following year's event was in Croatia. The program allows both adults and children to take classes, explore the city and meet incredible people. We were excited to go, but I was also very nervous. I had never been out of the country with the kids, and we had rarely traveled without Nate. My gut said we needed to go, but I also knew if I thought about it too long, I would back out. So, without overthinking it and with the encouragement of my Tia, I bought the plane tickets, booked a hotel and trusted the rest would work out.

Those days in Estonia, out of the country together for the first time, turned out to be one of the best trips we have ever had. From the plane ride to the medieval town to Estonia's unique restaurants and the quaint hotel where we stayed, that trip healed us in many ways. We saw castles and met brilliant authors and speakers that were working on changing the world. We listened to thought leaders in physics and science and spent time exploring old shops and museums off small cobblestone streets. We even went to a cat cafe, a place where you could drink coffee while watching cats play. It was a strange experience, and if I am honest, one I would never do again. Spending ten days in the historic town of Tallinn with some of our closest friends was a gift. Most days and nights, we stayed out late, sitting around a table discussing life, spirituality and how to live our best lives.

During those few weeks, I met a lot of interesting and

intelligent people. We discussed deep and profound topics along with many weird and out-of-the-box ideas. Many of our late-night talks included how different people and cultures deal with fear, death and the journey through loss. Almost everyone seemed to have a unique story of heartache and openly shared how they navigated it.

Through those conversations, I began to examine my relationship with fear and my understanding of death. I knew I still had a lot of grief work to do, especially around the trauma I experienced the day Nate died. One thing I know about grief: it's stored in your body, even if you have pushed it out of your mind. Grief is a physical experience, a loss and a trauma that changes not only your soul but your cells and your body. When unimaginable situations happen to us, it changes the essence of who we are while also teaching us hard and important lessons. But grief must be acknowledged, physically experienced and then released for the transformation to take place. If we don't take these steps, it physically lodges itself into us and stays there until you give it the time and attention it deserves.

There was so much I hadn't yet been able to process, especially around the actual day that he died. And I knew those moments were loaded with trauma. Through all the talk therapy and bodywork I had done, I still wasn't able to fully remember many parts of the flight back from Jamaica, anything from the layover or the experience in the morgue. I knew they happened, but there was a distance and a numbness that was making me nervous. I could remember the terror, but after that, the details got fuzzy. When people asked me about the plane ride home, I would say, "It was awful, but I can't even remember where I had my layover. It's like it has all been blocked out." I knew those emotions were in me; they were just locked deep inside.

As I spoke about my pain, sadness and anger in Tallinn, people began to share some insights and tools they had used to deal with their own experiences. What struck me most during those discussions is that not one person thought I needed a break from my pain or sorrow. No one suggested I have a glass of vodka or take an Ambien or swallow a Xanax. No one told me to go away somewhere or find someone new to sleep with to numb my pain. Instead, each of them believed that the only way I would come through this as a healthy person was to lean even harder into the pain. Their advice was to find a way to bring it up, explore all of it and then let it go. The advice was simple, but it felt very hard to do. Feel it, accept it, embrace it, experience it and then ultimately integrate that pain into a new version of myself.

We talked about all the different types of therapy I was doing, and over the span of two weeks, multiple people asked if I was open to taking psychedelics to help me deal with my grief. I had never heard of this before and did my best to keep an open mind. At first, I had to pretend the idea didn't scare me to death. But if I am being honest, I was very skeptical and thought to myself numerous times, "this isn't for me." In my mind, psychedelics were something you did in college before a Phish show. And although many of my friends loved doing it when they were in their 20s, some of them had extremely scary experiences they never wanted to repeat.

My initial reaction was, "Nope, never going to do that!" I have always had an aversion to taking anything mind-altering. I even struggle with taking Advil PM. I spent my life being very uptight and had always been the girl who didn't want to lose control—I had a huge fear of something bad happening.

But after hearing more about the process—how you have an intention and carefully select the setting and the kind of insights you hope can come from it—I realized this experience of psychedelics was very different from a big night out on the town. The more I learned, the more I understood that when done in a safe, controlled setting with experienced facilitators, this could be an effective way to help people cope with PTSD, depression and trauma.

Still, even though I was beginning to understand the possible (and huge) benefits of this therapy, my fear and resistance didn't fade. My understanding of mushrooms and LSD came from movies and my brother's high school years. While I spent my teenage years underwater at swim practice, my brother enjoyed experimenting with mind-altering drugs and experiences. Maybe now wasn't the appropriate time for me to become "open-minded." I kept saying, "I have two kids to raise, and their father is dead. The last thing they need is to have me die after hallucinating on mushrooms and jumping off a bridge!"

Yet as I spoke to more people who had tried it, I became intrigued with the idea. What if it could help me access some of the deep pain and trauma? What if one experience could be equivalent to years of talk therapy? So, I started to do my research.

I read articles from Johns Hopkins that showed extremely favorable outcomes for people with depression or PTSD who had a properly administered experience with mushrooms. I listened to Tim Ferriss's podcast about the many people whose lives were changed by this therapy and why it had been taken out of medical circulation at the end of the 1970s. And lastly, I read *How to Change Your Mind* by Michael Pollan. His book eloquently, scientifically and anecdotally walks through these experiences in a balanced and honest way; it was the education I needed to feel much more comfortable with doing it myself. All the traditional ways of working through grief were helping me, but I knew I needed something more because, at times, the pain and sorrow still seemed insurmountable.

The final straw came in the form of a man named Jack that I met on one of the last days in Tallinn. It wasn't lost on me that he had the same name as my son. Jack was a one-of-a-kind guy and out there in so many ways. He was a world traveler and had experimented with mind-altering states and plants for a good part of his life. At first glance, I thought he was crazy. And in truth, he may have been. But after speaking to him one night, I felt something shift in my mind.

While we were at a group dinner, he shared stories of his travels, his experiences with mushrooms and the time he had sex in a thorn bush. He was odd, entertaining and admittedly, at times, very hard to believe. While he spoke, I rolled my eyes at least 400 times, but there was *one* thing he said in particular that stuck with me. At some point, I told him I was afraid to die while trying psychedelics, and he suddenly stopped me. He looked at me very intently and said quietly, "But don't you see? With all this fear, you are already dead. You are overcome with fear—you are stuck, paralyzed with anxiety and afraid of life. That's not living. That's death."

That one got me.

From then on, I knew that at some point in the future, I would have this experience. And I trusted I would know it when it showed up.

Almost two months later, I got a call from a friend I deeply trust. He said, "Hey, you ready for a journey?" Without hesitating, I said, "Yes."

Almost a year after I lost Nate, I was pulling up to a beautiful home in Laguna Beach, California, to try psychedelics for the first time. There were 12 people who would be participating; some were very close friends, and others were people I had just met that day. But we were all there for the same reason—to do some deep work on ourselves. We began by introducing ourselves and casually getting to know one another. Peggy and Bobby—the healers who were leading the event—brought us together in a circle to set intentions. I had spoken to Peggy over the phone a few days before. She had called to introduce herself, tell me about the process and better understand why I wanted this experience. She wanted to know what my intentions were and how I felt about it. Peggy is one of the most beautiful souls I have met, and I knew right away she was going to take care of us. She was lovely and calm, and I felt safe from the start. And the fact that her name was Peggy and her husband's name was Bobby soothed me on a deep level. For some reason I remember thinking, "Peggy and Bobby are names you can trust!" I guess I had expected their names to be more tribal or less mainstream, but in that moment, I was glad they sounded "regular" (whatever that means). After speaking to her, I knew this was the right thing to do.

The ceremony began in the living room, and there were candles everywhere. In the background, meditation music was playing, and the room was filled with feelings of love, trust and some healthy fear. As we sat in a circle, we each went around and shared why we were there. When it was my turn, I shared my story of losing Nate and said my hope was to grieve fully, work through the trauma around Nate's death and most importantly, to find a way to access him. I desperately needed to talk to and see him again because we never had the chance to say goodbye.

Everyone there had come to face their problems, not run away from them. Each one of us was willing and ready to look at ourselves fully and ask the big, hard questions. We each had a deep desire to heal wounds and gather insights around how we could do better in this life.

The medicine we would be taking had come from a shaman who was also a practicing doctor. He was born in Peru and had been doing this work for his entire life—he came from a family of healers who had used this medicine to treat people for centuries. What Peggy said to us before it started was what is always said in these ceremonies: "You will get what you need, but it may not be exactly what you want."

Peggy handed me the first pill; it went down fairly easily. She explained that it was simply an over-the-counter relaxant similar to a Calms Forte that you can get at a drugstore. I didn't feel much, but I did feel a little bit calmer. As we waited for the next dose, we sat around and talked about our lives, our families or anything that came up. We found places on the floor or couches to sit and relax and just be present.

After a few minutes, Peggy gave me the next pill. As I swallowed the pill, I felt the beginnings of a huge panic attack: I started breathing fast, my heart was racing, and I was furious at myself. I knew this was a mistake, and I wanted it out of me. I sat up and desperately waved my hand. I needed help; I was scared. Peggy arrived at my side and calmly said, "Kelsey, tell me what is happening." I cried and said, "I knew it! I can't do this—I'm not well! Something is wrong with whatever you gave me, and something is wrong with me."

She sat down right next to me and gently put one hand on my head and one on my heart and told me to slow my breathing down. "I just gave you a placebo—this is all in your head. Breathe. You are safe." As I began to breathe and relax with her by my side, my heart slowed down, and the panic subsided. She said, "I knew you might get nervous, so we started slow."

And for the first time in my life, I truly *knew* that a panic attack completely manifests in the mind but creates real physical sensations. It showed me how powerful our thoughts and emotions can be in a way I never experienced before.

Once I calmed down, she said, "Congratulations! That was great work. Now, here is what you will take next. This is the beginning of the journey; relax and go with it. You are safe."

I swallowed the pill and lay down on the floor next to some of my best friends. After about ten minutes, I felt the tears starting to slowly fall down my cheeks as the emotions and pain I had been holding in for so long began seeping out. I kept quietly asking people, "When will I know it's working?" And everyone kept saying, "You will know—just drop in." I had never done drugs, so I wasn't even sure what that meant—I just let go and let it all be.

And then I dropped in.

At that moment, time fell away, along with my ego. It was the first time in my life that I had no sense of people judging me or me judging them; it felt like freedom.

Right away, I felt the ball of deep, black grief stored in my stomach starting to move. "Emotions need motion," and that's exactly what I started to feel: a shifting of where and how that grief was stored. It was all the pain and fear I had pushed down since the moment I received the phone call telling me Nate had fallen and then, an hour later, that he was dead.

Grieving takes attention and time. I didn't have much of that. Too many people needed my full support. There were too many tasks I had to focus on. Raising two kids alone made it impossible to create the time and space I needed to fully grieve. It was too big and too scary to let all that out when I was responsible for the financial, emotional and physical health of an entire family.

There was no such thing as *Eat, Pray, Love* in my story. I couldn't abandon my life and head to Italy or rent a beach house. I had no time to sleep with some hot European stranger (although that did and still does sound very appealing). Because I had children (thank God), I found myself in the weeds of grief *and* regular life at the exact same time. Instead of *Eat, Pray, Love,* it was way more *Carpool, Cook, Cry*. Life went on, kids needed lunches packed and homework completed. It was near impossible to do a hard stop and really go *through* something.

But now, lying on the floor with people I trusted, was the first time I could give in. I let all the emotions come up, felt every single part of them and then began the process of letting them go. Within minutes, I was sobbing. I kept saying over and over again, "I loved him so much. I miss him so much!" The tears were huge, the pain was deep and the sorrow was immeasurable. But after a bit, the crying stopped, and I was quiet.

Suddenly, as if a scene changed in a movie, I was alone on the plane again, the one from Jamaica to California, flying back to my husband's dead body and to my kids who had just watched him die. On that day, it had taken me nine hours to get from Montego Bay to Los Angeles. I had been in shock for most of the flight, and because my fear and devastation had been so huge, my body and mind had blocked out the majority of the experience. It's unreal what our minds can do to protect us when we are dealing with traumatic events. We literally have a shut-down switch in our brain that says, "this is too much." Until that moment, I had very few memories of that plane ride.

With my eyes closed, I found myself sitting in the aisle seat again. I was alone on a plane, shaking and crying in a wet bathing suit. I was so terribly scared, and no one was looking at me or talking to me. I could feel exactly how I felt that day; it was a vivid reenactment that felt like it was happening again in that moment. I was completely present in the seat and knew I was heading back to tell my kids their father was dead.

The difference was, this time, I wasn't alone. As I cried and shook, I could feel angels from the Divine come and support me. Without saying a word, I was surrounded by love. My angels from heaven, my friends in that living room and a few other women from the group who intuitively knew I needed help sat down around me. I was in my own dream world, but I could feel all of them. They all showed up immediately at my side; many put their hands and arms around me. I could feel them all holding and supporting me as I sat on that plane and cried. I had an overwhelming sensation that, through their love and support, I could dive into that fear, feel it all, scream and cry and still be safe. I could feel myself healing and the pain moving out of me. They kept reminding me that I was strong, that I was never alone and that I was safe. Eventually, the tears stopped, the dry heaving ended and I got quiet again.

At some point (later, I found out it had only been five minutes), I sat up, opened my eyes and said, "Wow, that was hard. I'm so glad that's done!" The tears and the sobbing stopped immediately, and I was back to taking calm breaths and feeling a huge sense of relief. With my eyes open now, I was back into a normal reality and a regular living room.

I felt 100 pounds lighter; it was as if I had moved forward in some epic way. Peggy handed me some water, and I gathered myself, took a few sips and found a new place to lie down. Within seconds, I was back in the morgue at Harbor UCLA. It was the last place I had seen my husband, and I had been so afraid to see him—to see a dead person—that I wasn't sure I could even walk into that place.

Now I was there again, kneeling next to him and

stroking his face. I could feel his stubble. I kissed his face, and just like I had done nine months ago in real life, I climbed on top of him, wrapped my arms around his neck, and cried. I looked into his face and kissed him and told him how much I loved him. I was experiencing it all as if I were there again, only this time, I was watching myself do it from above. It was as if I were watching a movie of a girl named Kelsey saying goodbye to her husband named Nate.

I kept screaming, "No one should have to say goodbye to the love of their life in a morgue!" Again, by this time, people were around me, holding my hand or touching my face and saying, "That was so hard—you are so brave." And I just kept telling Nate over and over again, "I loved you so much. You were the best ever. It's okay—we are going to be okay." And then one of my close friends came up and whispered to me, "What a gift you just gave him."

Then that moment was over, and all I felt was overwhelming pride for the courage it had taken me to do that —followed by enormous relief from knowing I didn't have to do it again. I felt it all, I experienced it all, and then I felt peace. It was as if I had lived through it again, but instead of storing it in my body, I was able to process it and, in some ways, release it. I knew it would always be in my mind and my heart, but the medicine helped me move it *through* my body. Because of that, I now can remember that day without the numbness and pain. I now have the ability to look back and find gratitude for the ability to see him and say goodbye, even if his soul had already begun its transition.

My breath slowed down again, and a calm passed over me. I felt a great release and an overwhelming sense of gratitude. I got up, had some water, talked to a few people, and then took a minute to be quiet. I supported some other people in moments they were going through and then sat down on the couch. As long as my eyes were open, I felt like I was in my "regular" reality, but once I closed my eyes, I was back in another realm.

There was one last big grief moment that I needed to process. Anger was a stage of grief I had yet to experience because the sadness had been so big. But as I lay there, all the rage that had been inside me since he died came forward. With my eyes closed, lying on the couch, I yelled, "Who leaves someone with two kids to raise alone? Why did he make me a widow at 40?!" I was so loud and angry that a friend eventually stepped in and took me upstairs.

He was one of Nate's best friends and knew me very well. He had made a couple of these journeys before and was more adept at navigating the experience. He said kindly, "Okay, Kels, it's time to move on. Use this opportunity to talk to Nate. What do you want to say to him?" Immediately I started apologizing for all the times I had hurt him or done something wrong. He interrupted and said, "How is this helping? How does beating yourself up serve you or Nate?" I realized it didn't, but I wasn't even sure where to start. Then he said, "Ask Nate what he wants to show you. Call for him and tell him to share with you what you need to know."

And that is when my mind exploded.

I called for Nate, and there he was, immediately right in front of my face. It was unbelievable, and to this day, I can still access that feeling of being reunited with his soul. It was so joyful and so satisfying that I just kept on crying. It was *so* good to be back with him.

The first thing he showed me was our kids. He said, "Look over there!" and pointed to the left. There stood my beautiful children, Jack and Addison. But they weren't nine and 12—they were adults and were dressed like characters from *Game of Thrones*. They appeared to be actual warriors, and they both looked stunning. Nate said, "You don't need to worry about them. They were born for this moment and meant to be ours."

The next insight was that I had called for Nate in college, and he had shown up *for me*, not the other way around. Finally, it made sense. My whole life I thought I was serving him, but in reality, he was serving me. He had never particularly wanted to get married or have kids, but he did it because I asked him to, and with each step, he had fallen in love with the life we created.

I asked him about the feeling I had for many years, deep in my soul, that he was always going to leave me. He said we often talked about death because we were preparing for this moment. Most couples didn't discuss what would happen if one of them died, but it was a conversation we had multiple times. Nate used to say,

"You would be a terrible nurse! I never want to get sick with you!" And we would laugh because it was true. I had a lot of great traits, but patience was never one of them. He reminded me of what he used to say after we prayed each night. He would look at me and say, "You know, I can't wait to get to heaven." And I would respond, "Really? I have no desire to rush there." But now it made sense; his soul had come down to serve, and his time here would be short.

Then he told me, "I took on the body of a football player even though I didn't like it, and it was hard for me. Football was a way for me to be valued in our culture so I could sneak into people's hearts—I didn't have to prove my manliness because, in our society, football made me automatically respected." Basically, he was free to touch people's hearts in ways that might not have been available to him if he had traveled through life in a different body. His favorite part about being a football player had been talking to other people about God, especially people who had different beliefs.

At that moment, I thought back to every time Nate would stand in front of the bathroom mirror or the one by the closet and ask, "Hey Babe, is this how I *really* look?"

"Yes, exactly!" I would tell him.

He would shake his head in disbelief. "That is so weird, because how I feel on the inside doesn't match what I look like on the outside!"

I smiled, thinking of him saying that.

Then came the most impactful moment of this experience. It has fundamentally changed the way I understand death. When I told Nate how much I missed his body, his arms and his face, he said, "Watch this!" and then he simply dropped his entire "body" in front of me. I saw it fall onto the ground, almost like the dirty clothes you take off at the end of a long day. And then all that was left was his spirit. It was light and funny and skinny, and he was filled with so much energy.

His spirit took me by the hand, and we flew fast around the universe. "Let me show you how to play!" he said to me. "Let me show you how to have fun!" He said he had tried to show me how to interact with our kids when he was on Earth and how to have his ability to be present in the moment. That was why he never checked his email or voicemail when we were on vacation and why he took his time with everything. He wasn't of this world for long, so he knew a lot of that stuff just didn't matter. He knew that the importance of fishing with his kids far outweighed any corporate email.

He still wanted to show me what it looked like to have fun. He said, "It's not complicated—all you have to do is be where you are. What you are feeling right now is what it feels like to live in the present moment. Remember this feeling, and you'll know when you're in it."

I asked Nate what the kids needed from me, and it was like they were speaking through him. Addison asked for kindness and patience. She told me she needed me not to rush her, to take care of her soul and speak to her kindly. Behind her tough exterior, she said, she is a very sensitive person. Jack needed time with me to connect calmly. He needed *real* time with me, the kind of time he used to have with his father. He said, "Dad was showing me how to be a man, a present man. He taught me how to sit in the quiet space and truly listen to people." After I watched Jack's memorial speech, I realized that was one of the gifts they both gave me. As Jack spoke in front of all those people, I knew that Nate had done his work and that Jack was going to be okay. Now all I needed to do was show up and love him.

The next morning we participated in an Integration, which was led by our facilitators. An Integration allows you to begin to process and understand what you experienced during the Journey. While sitting in the living room and drinking coffee, we each shared the insights and lessons we had learned from the night before. Those final hours were filled with connection, support and encouragement from the group.

Those two days were some of the most transformative and enlightening experiences of my life.

That Journey and what I learned continue to impact my life. I gained a deep belief that Nate is still with me and that I have access to him. I found trust that even on the hardest days, we were going to be okay because there was a much bigger plan at work. It didn't mean that I didn't miss Nate or feel deep sadness anymore; it just meant I had more hope that there was magic in the missing. The magic came from knowing I got to experience that pain because I was lucky enough to love. It was magical because as I leaned into the pain, I began to transform and expand. Grief changed me in so many ways, and almost all of them made me a more compassionate and connected person. The magic showed up in how suddenly I was connected to a stranger on the streets, simply because I could see in their eyes that they too had lost something or someone they loved. The magic was that I realized I was never alone.

EIGHTEEN
CONCUSSIONS & CRYING

"The truth is rarely pure and never simple."
- Oscar Wilde

One morning in March of 2019, I sat down at my computer with a warm cup of coffee. Everyone was still asleep. I took a sip and reflected on the previous year and a half. It felt like we were finally in a good place. The kids were doing well in school, and I was back at my job. Life was different, but it wasn't all bad.

I opened my email and sifted through messages. As I scrolled down, I saw the name Lisa McHale, who was the Director of Family Relations at the CTE Center at Boston University. I swallowed hard and stared at the screen. I had been waiting for this email for a long time, but as the months passed, I had put it out of my head.

My stomach dropped, and I took a long breath. I dreaded what I might learn, but it was also a part of Nate's story that I needed closure on.

I clicked on the message.

Lisa McHale
RE: Nate's Case
March 7, 2019

Hey Kelsey,

Can you give me a call when you have a sec?

Thanks,
Lisa

I called her immediately.

"Hi, Kelsey," she said. "I'm sorry this took so long. We wanted to make sure we had looked at everything."

I thanked her for her help, and she continued, "After doing every test and analysis we could, both from a clinical and a pathological perspective, I want to tell you that Nate did indeed suffer from Chronic Traumatic Encephalopathy. And at the time of his death, his disease had progressed. Based on his brain tissue, he was suffering from Stage II or III CTE. I'm so sorry."

I had to sit down and let the news sink in. I felt sick. A broken heart and a broken brain—how could that be?

The severity of CTE is grouped into four categories. Stage I is the least severe, and symptoms include headaches, loss of concentration and memory. Stage IV is the most severe, and it presents with language deficits and psychotic symptoms, as well as motor deficits. Individuals who are diagnosed with Stage II CTE can suffer from depression, mood swings and memory loss. Those with Stage III can frequently develop more acute symptoms than those that are evident in Stage II. According to Boston University, "75 percent of the people studied with Stage III CTE were considered 'cognitively impaired.'"[1] When Aaron Hernandez died, he was diagnosed with Stage III, and Junior Seau died with Stage II CTE.

I felt like the world was spinning. How could my sweet husband have died with lesions all over his brain?

"Next, we'll set up a call with your family and Dr. McKee," Lisa continued. Dr. Ann McKee was the lead researcher on Nate's case and is a leader in the field of CTE and post-traumatic neurodegeneration. She has been instrumental in changing public awareness regarding the lasting effects of concussions, subconcussions and blast-related injury.

After we hung up, I sat there and cried. I cried for Nate, and I cried for the kids and me. I couldn't believe he had been so sick.

I waited about an hour, and then I called Nate's father, then his brother and finally his mom. Each conversation was brutal and ended in tears. This news felt heartbreaking on every level. The man we all loved so much had suffered silently for so long.

It's hard to put into words how I felt that day. There were so many different emotions I struggled to reconcile. The hardest part was comparing the diagnosis with the man I had loved for so long. I felt a huge sadness that he had been hurting, and I didn't know. I also felt guilt that he carried this disease by himself and regret that I hadn't been more aware. I beat myself up for conversations we had where he seemed confused and I got mad. And I also felt relief, for him and for us, that we didn't have to spend the rest of his life taking care of him or watching him deteriorate, which would have been his worst fear.

Later that week, we all joined a conference call with Dr. McKee, and she explained the study process and the diagnosis. She answered all of our questions, and afterward, we received the official email with Nate's autopsy results.

PATIENT'S NAME: Hobgood-Chittick, Nate AUTOPSY#: XXXX
DATE OF DEATH: 11/11/2017
DATE BRAIN RECEIVED: 03/28/2018 FROM: Los Angeles, CA
FINAL DIAGNOSES:
1. Chronic Traumatic Encephalopathy (CTE), *Stage II-III*
Comment: The brain had been previously sectioned, and only fragments were received. No abnormalities are noted. Multiple perivascular CTE lesions are present in the

superior frontal, inferior frontal, and left frontal cortices. There is mild neurofibrillary degeneration of the locus coeruleus, substantia nigra and nucleus basalis of Meynert. There is mild neurofibrillary degeneration of the medal temporal lobe structures. These changes conform to Chronic Traumatic Encephalopathy (CTE), Stage II-III (out of a possible IV, with IV being the most severe).

I have deliberated over including this chapter in the book. Can't I just tell the story of his beautiful life? Do I need to mention why and what contributed to his death or the awful state he and our family would have been in if he was still alive?

It didn't take me long to realize that the answer to that question was yes.

I don't hate football, and I'm not condemning the NFL; I am sharing a personal story about a man I loved who chose to play football. Because of that choice, he was given many gifts and opportunities, but he also paid a huge price. I know he loved football, and yet I am certain he wouldn't have chosen to die for it.

On most days, I tell myself that Nate died because his time was up, that his life ended at the exact right time, in the exact right way. I believe that when he had a massive heart attack in front of his kids, angels showed up right away to usher him home. I also believe he died on 11/11 around 11 am because that is a highly spiritual time, and he was a very special man. I love believing that Nate left this Earth at 42 because he had done everything he had come here to do. In what is typically half a lifetime, he had managed to share all his gifts and change the world for the better. So, on that day, it was time for him to go home.

God, I love that story. That version feels so good. And when I tell it that way, I feel a peace and acceptance that transforms the pain of losing him into the gratitude of knowing him.

On my best days, this is the story that I tell myself.

But then there are the facts: the medical reports, the brain autopsy, and the sport he played that undeniably had a large role in his death.

There are aspects of life that simply aren't black and white, "good" or "bad." We make thousands of decisions each day that ultimately create the stories of our lives. And when you change one, you change everything.

No one can deny the gifts that football gave us. But in spite of all those blessings, football ultimately took more than it gave.

I'm not speaking for Nate on this. I did that enough during our marriage, and he would kill me if I tried to now. But I am speaking for myself, my children and his family.

No matter how much I want to focus on the gifts, I cannot ignore the long-term effects this sport had on my husband and may continue to have on some of the brightest, kindest and most talented men I know.

Nate would say that he had a love/hate relationship with football, and I think that is true for a lot of players.

The people he met and the experiences he had enriched his life in so many ways. But I also know that Nate and other players pay a price for what they put their bodies through. Some may live in pain for the rest of their lives, and others may end up disabled. Many will die early or live in ways that become unrecognizable.

We now know the price Nate paid, and it was enormous.

Nate died because of his heart disease, but in some ways, it's a blessing that he didn't live longer. Nate was the most incredible, connected man I had ever met, and to watch him live with Stage III brain disease would have been unbearable.

At times watching him in the years before his death was hard. Many of those closest to him knew something was wrong, but we couldn't identify it. There was a distance and sadness to him that was hard to understand. He would get confused, and at times extremely tired and overwhelmed. It could have been because of work and family, but I knew in my heart that it was something different.

One of the biggest changes I noticed was in his decision-making ability. There was a look in his eyes I had never seen before. It was like he was far away and unsure of what was going on, like he was in a trance. While prepping for a cookout the summer before he died, he drenched the grill with lighter fluid, turned it on and set fire to our new wood fence. He got upset more easily and seemed to struggle in social situations that used to be easy for him. Alarm bells were going off inside my head. But because the changes were gradual and probably because I didn't want to see them, I didn't say anything.

But when we got the report, I understood that my gut was right, and something had been very wrong.

If not for his heart attack, he would have had to live with a severe and degenerative brain disease. In this one instance, I will speak for him: I know he would rather have died than live that way.

Were we saved in some way? I will never know what it would have been like to live with that diagnosis, so I choose to believe it was a blessing.

What I do know is that his heart disease is what killed *him*, but his brain disease would have killed *us*. We weren't lucky to lose this great man, but we were lucky we never had to see him suffer from CTE.

Over the past 20 years, football players have gotten bigger and faster. The hits are harder; the punishment to their bodies is deeper. And in some high-profile situations, we are starting to see some of these guys—who are making a lot of money—are walking away from it all. They know that the price their bodies are paying will outweigh the benefits the sport can give them.

Yet they are the lucky ones because they have the means to walk away. All across the country, kids as young as six are starting their football careers. Many believe football is their way out of poverty. They don't think about having lesions on their brains, or how their backs won't be able to bend, or what it would mean to be diagnosed with Parkinson's or early dementia. For too many kids, football seems like their only chance for a better life. But they may not fully comprehend the price.

Research on these injuries and the link between football and CTE is only beginning[2].

In the Collective Bargaining Agreement that was signed by both the NFL and the players union in 2011, the league agreed to provide compensation for players who suffered from injuries and neurological conditions that had been linked to their time playing football. Included in the original decision, the NFL concussion settlement identified the following diagnosis: amyotrophic lateral sclerosis (ALS), death with CTE (diagnosed after death), Parkinson's, Alzheimer's and Level 1 and Level 2 of neurocognitive impairment (early and moderate dementia).

But a few years later, a change was made that any player who died with CTE after April 22, 2015, would no longer qualify. That means no family of a player who dies with CTE will receive any financial compensation, including mine.

Because football gave us so much, I struggle to convey the mixed feelings I have about the sport. There is still so much love I have for the people we met and the opportunities it gave us.

But my mother-in-law does not; her feelings aren't mixed at all.

For years she has believed that we must take a deeper look at this sport and the effect it has on young men, kids in underserved communities and the society that values it so much. From the first time Nate played football at the age of 12, she was concerned about his health and safety. And she didn't just feel that way for him—she had that feeling for every child who played.

From her viewpoint, this is a much bigger issue than just a game. She looks at football from societal and economic perspectives. She is critical of the power and wealth divide in this country and is adamant that a society that still wants to watch grown men tackle and injure each other in a coliseum-like atmosphere is archaic. This sport heavily relies on the bodies and brains of the poorest and least privileged men and promises a way out for kids in communities who don't have many other options.

I have talked to many great players and world-class coaches who have a different perspective, many of them close friends of Nate. When I bring up his diagnosis or my feelings about CTE, they have similar answers. "Yes, there are clear dangers within the sport. Everyone knows that. But each man chooses to play, and each man can quit if he wants." They have a real argument, and it is one I agree with on many levels. But then I normally ask, "But if you took the money out of it, would anyone still play?" And that is when the discussion gets more complicated.

Nate started playing football in seventh grade. His mom often told me that he came home from school one day and literally begged on his knees to be allowed to play. His parents—educators at Harvard and Holy Cross—had no interest in football, but he wanted it so badly that they gave in.

Nate's sheer size and physical nature made football a sport he was naturally good at. It was obvious early on that he was going to excel. Playing for William Allen High School in Allentown was Nate's favorite time as a player; many of his best stories and memories were from those years. His mother never went to his games; she even skipped the Super Bowl. She tells us now that on some deep level, she always knew that if Nate played football, it would harm him greatly. But she also believed stopping him was nearly impossible.

Nate's sentiments about football were clear: he hated practice, his body hurt terribly, he was always trying to gain weight and he loved being a part of a team. He loved the way those games created community and loved the coaches and players he met along the way. Nate loved playing and watching football, but I assume there was also an internal battle between gratitude for the game and an awareness of what it was taking from him.

Nate was the guy that took a ton of hits in practice. He made the super-talented men try harder, simply because they didn't want him to outwork them. He quickly learned how to ignore pain and to push through everything that physically hurt him. He just stopped caring and said, "This is the price I pay for playing this sport." He knew this career was short, and he wanted to make the most of it.

He also wanted to save money because he told me, "If we can save, it will allow us to do so much." And so, he saved, and he took hits, over and over again, starting in high school until the last snap he took in the NFL. And when it was all over, he was completely relieved and also exhausted. Everything on his body hurt. He suffered from terrible acid reflux, a side effect from taking too many anti-inflammatory pills. His ankle had pins in it, his shoulder killed him, he got dizzy when he stood up, and he had severe sleep apnea. His toes looked like mangled tree limbs. Some mornings he couldn't bend his fingers, and he lost his breath at weird times. Many days he said his brain was "foggy," and he was tired a lot.

How do you unwind a life and decide what to keep and what you wish you could have changed? I've thought about that a lot ever since the day I sent Nate's brain to the Concussion Legacy Foundation in Boston. And I still don't have the answers. It's complicated, but his story is true and important. I want the conversations around football to continue, I want to see young boys protected and I want dads to stay alive.

Football brings a lot of joy to a lot of people. But each time a football player steps onto a field for the love of their town and the cheer of their crowds, he is paying a price for that glory.

Sometimes the price may be bigger than they expected.

NINETEEN
GRATITUDE & JOY

"For certain is death for the born and certain is birth for the dead; Therefore, over the inevitable thou shouldst not grieve."

-Bhagavad Gita

Before Nate died, I would have classified myself as a "hands-off *and* overly worried parent." Not a combination I would recommend. I panicked when they got a fever or a cavity. I got overly involved with everything and tried to make each moment a teaching opportunity.

"Hey Mom, I got in trouble today," one of them might say. "The teacher said I was talking, but I promise I was just answering a question and my—" And then, before they could even finish, I was coaching, correcting or telling them how to deal with it. Turns out that type of approach makes kids hesitant to share. Who knew?

After Nate died, it got worse—whatever they said, I wanted to make it better. I tried everything, threw all the rules out the window and gave them anything they asked for.

But it wasn't helping; I was making a hard situation much worse.

So, at some point, I stopped. I stopped trying to teach them or fix them or reframe the story for them. I started to listen, which isn't a skill that comes naturally to me. My brain screams, "But I have so much to share! I can help you!" I come from a long line of bad listeners. My dad tends to check out, and my mom gives continuous unsolicited (though brilliant) advice. On the flip side, my Grandaddy and Tia are great listeners; I didn't get that trait, but I did get my Granddaddy's nose, which is a shame.

Many days, it felt like a Herculean task to keep quiet. There were times when all I wanted to do was jump in and interrupt, but I knew I couldn't. The one who helped me the most during this time was my father-in-law. He was one of the best gifts I got from marrying Nate. He's wise, kind, smart and the best listener I have ever met. He has honed this skill over his lifetime as a Lutheran minister in churches, colleges and shelters, where he has served those who needed to be heard the most.

I called him one day in tears, overwhelmed by the task of raising these kids alone and shepherding them through this pain. He listened, then he reminded me of a conversation we'd had about a year before, sitting on the porch at their Maine cottage overlooking the Penobscot Bay. I had told him I had an overwhelming desire to control everything. After I finished speaking, he took one of his long, drawn-out pauses and then asked, "How does the mantra 'I am not responsible' feel?"

I sat with it and realized it felt like—well, *relief*. Huge and overwhelming relief. It was a novel idea, especially given my lifelong tendency to try to help and fix in all my relationships. To say "I am not responsible" was a huge risk.

Then I asked him, "You mean I'm not responsible for my children's pain, your heartbreak, or for making this all work out perfectly?"

He paused; I could feel him searching for the right response. He then quietly said, "You aren't responsible. Not for any of it."

The relief that sentence gave me was a game-changer. It was what I needed to hear more than anything.

It took me a long time after Nate died to begin integrating this new insight. I began to slow down and listen more. It was a skill I had never practiced, but this experience gave me plenty of opportunities to learn what a gift listening can be.

Like many mothers, I had prayed for my children since the day they were born. I asked that nothing bad happen to them. "Dear God, please let them make friends—avoid a shark attack—not choke on a grape—not break an arm—not drink and drive."

I wanted their lives to be joyful, easy and filled with as little pain as possible. In a perfect world, kids don't have to suffer big problems or experience great pain. But it wasn't until they lost their dad that I realized I couldn't make everything better.

That was the hardest and most liberating lesson of my life.

THOSE BRUTAL NIGHTS during the first few years were the perfect time to practice relinquishing this responsibility. I had spent so many nights staring at the ceiling, holding my daughter as she screamed and thinking, "This is unbearable. I can't do this much longer."

By accepting the idea that I wasn't responsible for fixing my kids' pain, I opened up a portal that allowed me to access Nate directly. Magically when I stepped back, he stepped forward. When I was calm and just witnessing the moment, I could feel him all around me. Whether I was in meditation or just sitting with the kids quietly supporting, I wasn't alone. The hair on my arms stood up, and it felt like there was electricity around my body. I knew he was with me because he had become *love itself*. When I was still, I could tap into mystical and magical moments with the Divine, and Nate surrounded me with his presence.

In those moments, I heard a whisper. It came from my *heart,* not *my head*—I felt it more than I heard it.

"You are doing it. Breathe" or "You got this. Just be with them. You are just what they need."

Many times, I would ask Nate questions. The answers would come immediately.

"How do I help them?" I cried.

"Just listen," I would hear. "They are right where they need to be."

When I was scared or frustrated, I would scream at Nate, "This is too hard!"

And immediately I would feel the message, "Stop talking—slow down."

And that's how I always knew it was him. All he ever wanted was two things for me:

1. Stop talking
2. Slow down

It gave me great peace to know his advice in this realm *and* in the Divine remained consistent.

As the months and years went by, I kept getting better at the single parent/widow gig. I was learning how to live this life in new ways, and I was proud of who I was becoming. Through our experience as a family, I learned that the hardest part about grief work was that it was so personal and unpredictable. Although we were grieving together, each person's path was unique. Jack is task-oriented and works hard at everything he does. He faces life, sports and school with a clear plan and a strong work ethic. And that was how he approached dealing with his father's death.

Addison was younger when he died, but when she turned 12, everything she had pushed down began to surface. The sweet little girl she had been a few years ago became more emotional and angry about losing her dad. Whenever I would ask how she was feeling about him or start to share memories, she would say, "Please don't talk about it; it makes me too sad!" I was scared because I could see her pushing those feelings down, and I prayed that one day soon, she would feel safe enough to experience them and move them out.

One night, after dinner with a man I had started dating, tensions were running high. When we got home and I put her to bed, she told me, "I don't like him, and I don't need a new person in our life." I told her I understood how she felt but couldn't promise her anything would change.

"Can you tell me why it's so hard?" I asked.

With tears in her eyes, she said, "Because when I see him, it reminds me that my dad is gone, and I hate that feeling!"

Something switched in that moment and whatever she had ignored or locked away began to surface. She was *so* furious with me and in so much pain. Finally, she just broke down.

"Mama, I miss Dad so much," she cried. "I feel like I am going to throw up. I hate everything right now," she whispered as we laid together in bed. As she spoke, I just rubbed her back and tried not to say a word. The more she shared, the angrier she got, and at some point, she started yelling and screaming. Then, about five minutes later, she began to cry.

But this time, it was a different type of cry. This cry was so deep and painful it sounded like it came from her soul. For the first time, when the deep pain of losing her dad came up, she didn't get scared or swallow it. This time she leaned into it and courageously let it wash over her.

Once she gave into it, she cried non-stop for an hour. At some point, she threw up in the bathroom. It was all coming out. We walked outside so she could ground herself in the grass, and she began to dry heave in the yard. The whole time I didn't say a word. I just rubbed her back and told her she was strong, and I was with her. At some point, Jack came to check on both of us. I told him she was missing Dad and working through that grief. With his wise, loving face, he turned to me and nodded. "You're an amazing mom," he said. Then he gave me a hug and went back to bed.

It took a few years for that deep pain to surface and for her to allow herself to feel it. At 12, she was now clear that her dad was gone, what happened was real and it hurt like hell. Watching her let the waves roll over her was painful and scary, but I knew it was also a gift.

Finally, her breathing slowed down, and she collapsed on her bed. She was exhausted, drenched in sweat and shaking. With her brown eyes still wet, she looked at me and said, "Mama, what was that? What just happened?"

"That was you letting pain out, of missing Dad and feeling it all." We held hands and both stared at the ceiling for a while before she replied, "God that was awful. I hated it, and I never want to do that again."

I gave her a hug and told her how courageous she was and how much I loved her. When I went to give her one last kiss before bed, she said, "Mama, I feel so much better. Thanks for being here and helping me."

I squeezed her hand and looked into her eyes. "I love you sweet girl. You are so strong."

She smiled back and whispered, "I'm okay now."

TWENTY
FLY FREE

"One of the best teachers in all of life turns out to be death."

– Michael Singer, *The Untethered Soul*

The last Halloween that Nate and I spent together was the first time in 15 years we had dressed up as a couple. We went as Baby and Johnny from the movie *Dirty Dancing*. I carried a watermelon (from the bridge scene, if you've seen it), and he wore a tight black T-shirt that said, "She had the time of her life, and she owes it all to me." At the end of the night, when the DJ saw our costumes, he started to play the movie's theme song, "Time of My Life." Nate and I did our best to attempt the lift from the final dance scene in the movie, and it was a huge hit. The crowd at the party cheered, and afterward, he and I walked home holding hands. It was a wonderful October evening, and we kept remarking on how happy we were in our lives and with each other. He died 10 days later.

Almost two years after that, I was driving to the beach for my morning walk, and I began crying, thinking about what we had and what we would miss. I wanted to see him and hug him so badly. And then, in that exact moment, the theme song from *Dirty Dancing*, "Time of My Life," began to play on the radio. I dried my eyes and smiled to myself. He was making it so obvious for me.

When I parked at the beach, I sat there and cried a little more.

"Nate, I miss you so much, and I'm so sorry you had to die," I said out loud to him. "But I'm so grateful you aren't sick and are at peace. I'm blown away at how strong we are and how great our life is. We are doing things we never dreamed of doing. Thank you for setting us up to have spectacular lives. I know it must have been hard to die. We miss you, and we love you."

And then I heard, deep in my heart, "Sweetie, it wasn't hard for me to die. The hard part was for you to choose to keep living. I love you."

Nate was gone, and he wasn't coming back. His brain had been autopsied, and his body had been cremated. There was no chance we would ever see him again, and even if he were still alive, life would have been extremely hard for all of us. How could I make sense of all this? Where could I find peace with the pain? How could I continue to accept this life exactly as it is?

I wanted to look at death in a totally different way, to challenge my thoughts around what happens when someone dies. I wanted to maintain a relationship with him. I trusted my connection, but I also read a lot of books that supported my gut feeling. *Home with God* by Neale Donald Walsh and *Untethered Soul* by Michael Singer both expanded my views on death. I don't think of death as an ending. I think of it as a transformation. If energy cannot be created or destroyed, his soul has to be somewhere. And I believe it's nearby. In my mind, when I picture people dying, I see them unzipping from their bodies, their physical expression, and flying free into the beauty of the Divine.

If I can talk to God, I can definitely talk to Nate.

I believe everyone goes to a place filled with love. Religion doesn't matter; God welcomes us all home. I don't think God has a lot of rules; it doesn't make sense to me that he would work that way. Too many rules and regulations would make Heaven seem like a country club. I believe good people experience Heaven on Earth, and the same goes for Hell. That happens here in this life, not in some faraway land. I believe that after you die, you become a part of everything. The people we love are always around us. They show up everywhere, in hummingbirds and flowers, great songs and heavenly sunsets.

I know one thing: Nate isn't gone. I don't know where

that kind, beautiful soul is, but I trust it's somewhere wonderful. Nate's body was his "Earth suit"—and it served him well until it didn't. For the rest of my life, I'm going to keep trying to find new ways to access him and continue our relationship.

Nate's death is a continual reminder for me to stay aware of the mystical and magical and beauty of life. His death reminds me that I don't have to have all the answers, and I don't have to understand everything. All I need to do is have faith and trust all is well.

I don't just want to come to terms with Nate's death; I want to find a way to come to terms with all deaths, including my own and that of my children. I think that might be the secret to living. It doesn't mean walking through life without caution, or good health, or a healthy dose of fear—it just means trusting that on some deep level all is well.

It turns out that Nate and I are getting along famously in this new setup. We communicate all the time, and yes, I still do most of the talking. Our relationship is similar to the one I have with God. When I talk to either one of them, I am filled with joy, and they make me feel safe. And just like God, Nate always answers me. I just have to pay attention to his signs.

TWENTY-ONE
MOVING FORWARD WITH HOPE

> *"May your choices reflect your hopes, not your fears."*
>
> - Nelson Mandela

I needed to write the final chapter, but it seemed each time I wanted to put a period on this part of the journey, everything would change. Each time I thought I had it figured out, that I had "made it" or was on solid ground, a new experience would swirl it all around again. It's been over three years since he died. Six months ago, I remember thinking, "You did it! Time does heal, and now we can begin living again. Things are looking up!"

And then a global pandemic hit the world. Suddenly everything turned upside down again, but instead of it just being in my house, it was happening all over the world. Social injustice became the focus of conversations. Kids stopped going to school. Masks became normal and economic devastation was affecting people and communities all around the globe.

I never saw that coming.

So how does this story end? How does any story about life really "end?" I think the answer is that there is no real ending, but instead, a lot of new beginnings.

For a while I thought maybe there was some destination, some magical day when it wouldn't hurt so bad. But that hasn't happened yet. I keep waiting for the grief to take a long vacation, go away and just leave me alone for a day, a month or a year. It turns out, at least for me, that grief might be a lifelong friend. I am trying to accept it, see its gifts and have peace with the fact that we may travel together for a while.

Grief reminds me of my humanity. The pain you feel when you lose someone is universal, and that feeling keeps me connected to others. Loneliness wasn't something I was familiar with before Nate died, but now we are quite close.

Many days, I still have a deep longing to go back in time: talk to him, hug him or just feel his hands. I have emotions I didn't have before: sorrow, regret, emptiness. And these emotions have changed me, and mostly for the better. I have a deeper appreciation for the human experience. I'm definitely not on autopilot anymore. In contrast, my life feels brighter, more intense, more *here.*

My grief connects me to my great-grandmother. She was a brilliant woman living in Paris, who fell in love with an American soldier and had two babies with him. But after the war, he left her to go back to the States, and she was alone, raising two kids. She never remarried. I feel her pain, and I recognize her strength. I feel connected to both of my grandmothers; one was abandoned by her father at the age of four, and the other lost her husband in the war. I feel their sadness, and I recognize their faith.

I have learned more in the last three years than I did in the previous 40. When Nate died, I had the unique opportunity to start over. Moments for immediate or instant growth may only happen once in a lifetime. I got to think about what I loved and what I wanted to let go.

Fear is the biggest part of me that I want to leave behind. I know that on the other side of my fear is freedom. I'm working to come to terms with what I know is the truth: life is hard, people die, kids get sick and relationships end. And slowly I'm making progress. I'm still afraid, sometimes completely terrified, but now I call it out and welcome it into my life, and then keep going.

My mantra around fear is:

Hello Fear! I see you, and I hear you, but we are doing this anyway. You can come along for the ride; just know that you're not the one driving."

Life is not linear, and neither is Grief; it's a million twists and turns that include a combination of big and little, hard and beautiful moments. The more I accept them, sit with them and experience them, the more magical my life gets.

I want to love again, share my life with someone again, and mostly, I want to laugh more than I cry again. I have enormous faith that all of that will work out. I am expecting it to end up better than my wildest dreams.

Grief ebbs and flows like the tides, and some days I'm not sure how to stay afloat. But what has changed is that now I know how to navigate those days. I pray, I meditate, I read, I spend time with friends and walk in nature. Those things all keep me above water and carry me along my way.

I used to think my job was to figure it all out—not anymore. I don't need to get anywhere because there is nowhere to go. Wherever I am right now, like it or not, is exactly where I need to be. I won't ever be done grieving, I won't ever have it all figured out and I won't ever write a final chapter.

Nate shows up through birds and music and messing with our Wi-Fi. I have peace that he is already at the place where I will go someday. I am in no rush to get there, but I look forward to pulling up a chair next to him and saying, "Well, that was rude, but it's so damn good to see you again. You won't believe how great things turned out—" I imagine him playing cards, enjoying a scotch and a bowl of peanuts. I see him at the table with my Granddaddy, Uncle Ken and my sweet grandmother VoVo. Life is good wherever those souls are.

Nate's story wasn't over when he died, and neither

was mine. We both just turned the page to a new chapter. A huge part of his impact and legacy started after he died. His death woke people up. They changed how they acted, they looked at life differently, they tried to do better. They quit drinking, they got in shape, they had deep conversations with their kids or began to love their partners better. My children grew up, found inner strength, got grit and became courageous. They experienced great loss and recognized it in others. Their hearts got bigger.

Finding a way to access Nate saved me. I refuse to live without him and am grateful that we have found a different way to connect. I still walk through life with him, and we raise our kids together. He's a part of all of us, and I'm grateful for everything. When he was alive, he loved me so well, and his leaving is the reason I came to understand my strength.

These days he often comes to me in dreams. A few months after losing him, I told my therapist that it broke my heart that I would never see him again.

"But you just said you can see him in your dreams, right?" he asked.

"Yes," I replied, "many nights he shows up when I call for him. It's so good to see and feel him in my dreams."

He paused for a moment and said, "So you *do* get to see him! Don't tell me that you're going to get picky about which realm he visits you in!"

I love that so much; it gives me great peace—and I'm not picky anymore.

EPILOGUE

11:11

In 1973, Nate's parents, Tom Chittick and Mary Hobgood, were newly married and looking for a place to vacation during their summers in Maine. They dreamed of buying a small cottage near the water where they could spend a few weeks each summer. For a teacher and a minister, money was tight, but their vision was clear. They wanted a cottage where they could bring their kids, relax and enjoy the natural beauty.

After searching for months, they found a humble, unfinished wooden cottage in a little town called Bayside. Bayside is a 19th-century Victorian cottage community in the heart of Maine, about 20 minutes north of Camden. The cabin needed work and was out of their budget, but when they stepped onto the small front porch and looked out at the breathtaking view of Penobscot Bay, they knew they had found their place. That day, they took out a mortgage for $7,000 and became the proud owners of a quaint summer cottage. It was their dream come true.

Once they had kids, the cottage became the one constant in their lives. Each summer, no matter where they lived or what was going on, they spent time together there as a family. It was their own little slice of heaven.

When I met Nate, he asked me if I wanted to join him at his parents' place in Maine. I could tell he was nervous, and I asked him why.

"You're the only girl I've ever brought with me," he said.

And so the year I turned 21, we drove to the cabin with his brother Luke in an old Volvo, listening to rap music by Tupac and Biggie Smalls.

Over the next 19 years, as our family grew, we went to Maine every summer. Even though we were living in California, we only missed two summers, and those were the years we had newborns. Our daughter was baptized by her grandfather in a tiny gazebo off the main road with a beautiful view of the water. Jack learned how to drive a boat with his dad in Penobscot Bay. It was a place filled with love. Many of our cherished memories as a family were made during those trips to the cottage.

Nate treasured everything about Bayside. He loved the smells, the community, and most importantly, his time on the water. Each night after the kids and I went to bed, Nate would walk down to the dock to sit with his thoughts. He would sit for hours, staring out at the water, which was only lit by the moon.

When Nate died, we all agreed the only place to leave his ashes was in Penobscot Bay.

IN JULY OF 2019, almost exactly 44 years after his parents bought the cottage, the kids and I returned to Maine to give Nate's ashes to the bay.

We spent a few days in Portland with his mom first, then headed up to the cottage. Bayside is about two hours north of Portland, and the drive is spectacular. We took two cars: one with Tia, Addison and me and the other with Jack, Luke, Tom and his wife Nicky. We were on our way to do one of the hardest tasks a family faces after losing a loved one.

As we were driving, I felt deep sadness and immense gratitude at the same time. I kept talking to Nate in my head, asking him for courage and support. There was a time when I wasn't sure I would ever be able to go back to Maine without him. For so long, I spent our time in Maine relaxing on the grass, reading the paper and walking around the small downtown; Nate had been super dad, the one in charge of the kids, teaching them how to catch crabs and pick blueberries and giving them the courage to jump off the high dock into freezing water. I needed to go back, but I had no idea how I would do this without him.

As we were crossing over the bridge that separates New Hampshire from Maine, we began the tradition we had done every year. Tom slowed down in the car ahead of me as if to remind me it was time. He called me on my cell.

"Is everyone ready to sing the Maine state song?"

"*Ready*!" the kids yelled. As we began to cross the bridge over the state line, we all sang together. The voices were terribly off-key, and only a few people knew the words, but I was smiling and singing, overcome with a sense of peace.

As we crossed the border, something drew my attention to their license plate. As I looked closer, I couldn't believe what I was seeing. I called my father-in-law.

"Tom, do you know what your license plate says?" I asked.

"No idea," he said. "It's Nicky's."

In Maine, a driver keeps their license plates no matter how many different cars they have in a lifetime. Nicky had gotten her plates back in the early 1970s, when they only had numbers and no letters.

I turned to Tia, "Can you please read the numbers on that license plate to me?"

I had chills all over my body as I tried to connect the dots that somehow converged on this moment in my life.

"One one one-one one seven," she read.

"Read it like a date," I said.

She paused and then said, "Oh my God. 11-11-17."

Nate died on November 11, 2017. And Nicky had

gotten those license plates 42 years ago, right around the same time Nate would have been born.

I believe in signs. I believe that God is always trying to send us messages and remind us that we are not alone. When I stay present and pay attention, I see signs everywhere.

There were so many events that had to happen for that license plate to be on that car as I crossed the Maine state line with my dear husband's ashes in the trunk. The chances were small—like one in never. There were births and deaths, marriages and divorces, kids and grandkids, so many twists and turns.

But in this one moment, it all came together. I knew there was magic in the missing.

NOTES

10. Helmets & Heartaches

1. https://www.ncbi.nlm.nih.gov/pmc/articles/PMC4098841/

18. Concussions & Crying

1. https://www.bostonglobe.com/metro/2017/09/21/symptoms-watch-for-four-stages-cte/Q1wniQOnQXH1bU8OibU3WJ/story.html
2. https://blogs.cdc.gov/niosh-science-blog/2012/09/06/nfl-brain-injury/

ACKNOWLEDGMENTS

Jack - You are the calm, the steady, the wise and loving energy in our life. Watching you grow up and being your mom is the greatest joy of my life. My job is to support you and stay out of your way because life has great and mighty plans for you. You are guided and guarded by God.

Addison - I have learned more from you than anyone else. Thank you for being my greatest teacher. Your wisdom and gifts are undeniable, and your inner light and certainty about who you are is inspiring. My life is infinitely better because you are in it. You are guided and guarded by God.

Michelle - In sixth grade, I knew you were the one. Before life partners were "a thing," you became mine. We have walked from LA to Florida at least 100 times over the last 30 years. Thank you for always being by my side and always living semi-next door. Life is good because you are in it. You are the Libra to my Cancer, the methodical to my speed, the practical to my emotional. We make a great team. And you are forever my best friend.

Tia - Every now and then, God creates a human that is pure love, someone who makes life better, who is always there, without judgment or pause. Your love has been a constant in my life, and your support and words always remind me that everything is going to be all right. The world needs more Tias. To the greatest aunt and godmother in the world, thank you for loving me so well.

Mom - I am the person I am because you are my mother. You are a force to be reckoned with, an Aries who knows what she thinks and will fight for the people she loves. Thank you for teaching me about the importance of independence, courage and finding my own voice. You have so much strength and continue to be a brilliant example of someone living life joyfully on her own terms. I love you very much.

Unicorns (Anne Marie, Cary, Laura, Neely, Kristen, Karin, Lise, Katie, Trina, Michelle, Ashley) - I'm not sure what I did to be given the honor of going through life with this crew, but it has been magical. A rare group of women with different views, different lives and different beliefs who have loved, supported and encouraged each other for over 30 years. Here's to our future and to living together in a row of condos on a beach in Florida. Of course, any current or future husbands are welcome—to visit. You are my people, now and forever.

Dad - Thank you for always encouraging me to live my best life. You have always trusted my path and believed in me. You are the true writer in the family, the one who expresses himself best on paper. You gave me my love of writing, comedic timing and the ability to find humor in everything.

Clegg - Having you as a big brother in childhood was great. Having you as a best friend as an adult is even better. Thanks for being the one person who truly "gets it." My life is better because of our conversations and our connection.

Steve - Love heals pain—this I now know for certain. You chose to walk a courageous, complicated and beautiful path with me in my darkest time. Your love and support brought me back to life, to living in the present and being excited about the future. You are a very special man and one of the great gifts of my life.

Tom - Now I can tell you that I married Nate partly because I would get to be your daughter. He was exceptional, but you set the standard from the start. The way you listen, the way you pause for understanding and the love you have shown me have changed my life. Since the day I met you, I have felt a connection that was deep and real. It's obvious that Nate learned how to be a father from watching you. I cherish our relationship, and you will always be one of the greatest gifts Nate left me.

Mary - A force to be reckoned with, a woman who inspires me to speak my mind, live my truth and feel it all. Your support has been enormous and unending. Your love for me has been complete, and your commitment to my joy has always been unwavering. You are always on my side, and I hope you know how important that is to me. I have learned a lot from you, but mostly what it is like to live with passion and strength. I am so glad to be your daughter-in-love.

Luke - I always thought I had something to teach you, but I was wrong. It is the other way around. You have faced the hardest, scariest and most insurmountable pain with courage, grace and a smile. Thank you for shepherding us through the first year and becoming the best uncle to my kids. Let's back half these next 40 years!

Chris - Thank you for introducing me to Nate; you started this whole amazing story. What you and Nate shared was beyond special, and we are all so lucky to have each other. Thank you for always being there for our family and for loving my kids as if they were your own.

October - The yin to my yang, my partner, my encourager, my stylist and one of the most beautiful humans I know, both inside and out. You continually push me to believe that I can have the life of my dreams. We were meant to be, and our journey together is written in the stars. Thank you for making my life better, brighter and way more fun. I would never have survived this without you.

Tony - You are one of the smartest and most generous humans I know. Your friendship is so honest and real. You don't let me get away with anything; no complaining, no feeling sorry for myself, no woe is me. From you I get encouragement, honesty and a friend who always asks me the hard questions. Thank you for always reminding me that I am stronger than I think and that my life begins on the other side of fear.

Beth - Thank you for teaching me how to write. Showing, not telling, is great advice, in books and in life.

Ajit and Neeta - Do the hard work, be authentic, tell your story. That is the next step. You both believed in me way before I believed in myself. Thank you.

El Segundo - The place you want to be if your husband dies. The love and support, the acts of service and friendship, all of it then and now. This town is a special place. Thank you for loving us and honoring Nate.

ABOUT THE AUTHOR

Kelsey Chittick is a writer, comedian and inspirational speaker. Over the past 14 years, she has performed stand-up comedy all over Los Angeles and speaks at events around the country. She is the co-creator of KeepON, an inspiring and humorous podcast that explores how our greatest obstacles turn out to be our greatest gifts.

Growing up in Florida, Kelsey was an accomplished student athlete—NCAA Championship individual and captain of the UNC women's swimming team. She was married to Super Bowl champion Nate Hobgood-Chittick.

For more about Kelsey and *Second Half*:
www.secondhalfbook.com